55

© 2018 McSweeney's Quarterly Concern and the contributors,
San Francisco, California. ASSISTED BY: Mieko Anders, Landon Bates,
Ellie Bozmarova, Rita Bullwinkel, Tasha Kelter, Lydia Oxenham. WEB
DEVELOPMENT: Brian Christian. PUBLISHING ASSOCIATE: Eric Cromie.
ART DIRECTION: Sunra Thompson. COPY EDITOR: Caitlin Van Dusen.
FOUNDING EDITOR: Dave Eggers. EXECUTIVE DIRECTOR: Amanda Uhle.
MANAGING EDITOR: Claire Boyle.

COVER AND INTERIOR ILLUSTRATIONS: Franz Lang.

Printed in the United States

DEAR McSWEENEY'S,

I am currently unemployed.

Sometimes I say I'm "on hiatus," because that's what they told me, but for a while it has been clear that the hiatus is never going to end. My wife—we'll call her Beatrice—has been tops. She knew I would be lying low for a while. I cook a lot to make up for being on hiatus.

The secret to a good puttanesca is to get drunk before you make it. You lose your garlic inhibitions and your red-pepper-flake inhibitions, just to name two of the inhibitions you lose. Make it with whatever you have in the cabinet. Plain anchovies.

I'll tell you a story about making puttanesca sober, and why it is a bad idea.

The last time I made puttanesca sober, I retrieved the anchovies from the pantry in their blue-and-white cardboard box. Of course, they're in a tin, but the tin is concealed in a blue-and-white cardboard box. And as I'm running my fingers over the surface of the blue-and-white cardboard box, I notice that it's a little distended. I think, Hmm, maybe that's the top of the tin, with the bumpy tab mechanism for the opening of the anchovy can.

So I slide the anchovy tin out of its protective cardboard and then I see: no! That was the *bottom* of the anchovy tin bulging ever so slightly. If I push it in, it pops back out with a little *poomp... poomp* sound. *Pa-poomp. Pa-poomp.* I think, This reeks of botulism!

Uh, *reek* is not a good word.

Botulism is indicated, I surmise.

But I drop the anchovies right into the pot anyway. With the onions, which were already caramelizing very nicely.

Liquid and all. Anchovy juice. The protective oil.

Oh! And the tab breaks off. Isn't that interesting? While I'm opening the anchovies. The tab breaks off, so I have to shake those anchovies out of their only partially opened tin. *Shake* them into the pot. Vigorously. Then I sniff the empty tin and think, I don't smell any botulism.

I know what you're thinking: This sounds exactly like cooking puttanesca drunk. And you're not wrong. But it was all the subsequent second-guessing that I could have avoided if only I had taken the trouble to get drunk.

I thought, If this... if these anchovies had botulism, wouldn't there be a... I mean, anchovies smell like anchovies anyway, so...

But I felt, never having smelled a quote "bad anchovy" unquote... I felt

I would know one if I smelled one.

But I didn't smell the anchovies themselves, which by now were already melting. I just love the way they melt into nothing.

I did sniff the tin and I found it satisfactory.

Then I said, "Oh, Beatrice, do you think these anchovies had botulism? They… the can was going *tha-thump, tha-thump. Pa-poomp, pa-poomp.* I know! I'll look it up on the internet."

I looked up "botulism." And, of course, one of the chief signs of botulism is a can with a bulging lid or seam.

Next I found an anchovy-specific website, which seemed to be run by an anchovy consortium. And *they* said that a little tin-bulging for anchovies is perfectly natural! But what else would they say? The bulging happens, according to the anchovy people, because of—I'm fabricating this right now because I can't remember the exact reassurances I was issued—a harmless bacteria present in the salt.

"An anchovy is a *semi*-preserved product," I believe is one almost-exact quotation from the anchovy website. "And so, on certain occasions, slight bulging may occur in the can."

The net result would have been the same whether I had cooked sober or drunk: Beatrice and I ate the suspect puttanesca and survived. But think about how much time and worry I could have saved by getting drunk. That's a practical household tip! And, as I say, the flavors are bolder when you cook drunk.

Beatrice came in from work last night and she was like, "Something smells good!"

Because I already had it cooking. That's a nice thing to do for a person if she has a job and you don't.

And then we ate it piping hot and Beatrice said she thought maybe it was my best.

So much hot pepper! So many capers and olives. And I tore so many parsley leaves from their stems, many more parsley leaves than I ever would have had the patience to fool with under more genteel circumstances. I don't put any fresh parsley in my puttanesca when I'm sober. Sober, parsley seems like too much work. I wash it too carefully. I pluck it too daintily.

Puttanesca is the enemy of subtlety.

Today I heated up the leftovers.

I was thinking, It's good to be on hiatus, because I already have, like, fourteen cloves of garlic in my body. I wonder how Beatrice's coworkers are doing.

So there's a flaw in my plan. I saw that being drunk and on hiatus can make you selfish, even when you think you're performing generous acts. I was transferring leftover spaghetti into the frying pan for lunch and a piece of onion lingered on the edge of the Tupperware. You should have seen this onion segment. It looked like a delicate folded fan, but, no, it wasn't folded. It looked like the tailfin of a beautiful car or an art deco brooch shaped like a scallop shell. You could see light shining through it but it was dyed pink with tomato or red wine.

There it was, in limbo between going back into the refrigerator and being eaten.

I knew it wouldn't be any more delicious than any other piece of onion. I knew it was crazy to consider saving it for Beatrice. I felt guilty about taking my stirring spoon and flipping that exquisite butterfly wing of onion into the sizzling oil, but I did it anyway.

Yours truly,

JACK PENDARVIS
OXFORD, MISSISSIPPI

DEAR McSWEENEY'S,
I've been giving people sheet masks. I hand them to friends, houseguests, dinner-party hosts, family members. My first book, *The Incendiaries*, was published in July 2018, and I've been traveling a lot to read from and talk about the novel; at bookstores, colleges, and festivals, I give still more sheet masks to booksellers, writers, and moderators. I take them to book clubs. If I'm seeing a friend for a drink, I'll bring a mask. I even gave one to my dermatologist, which, I think, puzzled him. Recently, after late-night karaoke, a close friend crashed at my place. The next morning, in full-on host mode, I asked if she wished to have a sheet mask, then stopped myself: I'd just recalled that she'd talked about not liking them. I told her as much.

"I don't like them, no," she said. "But I feel as though you were telling me something important by offering it as a gift, and I see that; I appreciate it."

What is it I was trying to tell her? Why do I wander around dispensing sheet masks like, as a friend recently called me, a hopped-up skin-care evangelist? For one thing, I like them. They're relaxing. I open the envelope, pulling out a thin single-use mask, filmy with liquid; I unfold the sheet; I mold it across my face until my reflection's covered, level, expressionless—and, like that, it feels as though I might also be able to smooth away all my usual fretting. I keep the mask on for fifteen, twenty minutes. I take it off, and it's left my skin visibly improved: shining, a little flushed, drunk with moisture. On the pleasure scale, it feels at least, I think, a third as relaxing as a massage, at a hundredth of the cost. It's like a glass of wine, but without the ensuing desire for a quick refill. Even the most skin-obsessed people I know will slap on a mask twice a day, at most. It has its own built-in endpoint! My god, I love masks.

But it's also true that they're good for one's skin, and that they can help us at least look as though we might be able to forestall time, change, dying. I grew up fanatically Christian. I lost the faith when I was in high school, a change so painful that, perhaps, it's always what I'm writing about. In addition to its other pledges, the faith promised life everlasting: to me, yes, but also to everyone else I loved, as well as to any of His children willing to follow the Christ who'd given His life for us. I'm still recovering from the blow of losing that promise. It's possible I'll never stop recovering. In the meantime, I dispense masks, and maybe it's as though I'm saying, *Don't go anywhere. Stay.*

Yours,

R.O. KWON
SAN FRANCISCO, CALIFORNIA

DEAR McSWEENEY'S,
It's the Friday before the Southern Festival of Books, and I'm writing to you from a plane to Nashville. I have decided this is the musical-theater episode of my book tour. A bridal party was doing a cheer routine in the lobby as we boarded in Boston, so expectations for Nashville are now very high. I have packed a cowboy shirt my husband doesn't like and I hope to wear it there—we will see. It's teal, which isn't a color I usually go for, but I like this one. The plane is a tiny fillet with wings, two seats on each side of that crooked aisle, and has NO SMOKING signs that look like they were printed in the '90s.

Behind me on this flight, a young woman in the emergency row is speaking directly to an older man about how she works with the first genetic testings for cancer drugs—not all of us can metabolize every drug, and our genetics determine which is best—and now she is explaining the Tagalog language. This is unexpectedly already one of the most important flights I've ever taken.

I admit to judging people when they are seated in the emergency row. I often sit in the row in front of it or behind it. I've noticed that the people seated there are often not truly equipped to take that door off even when they swear they are. I realize some people have hidden strengths. All the same, I often formulate a strategy for getting to the door should they fail. I like my life and will fight for it always. But I make a decision to trust this woman with my life.

And then we take off and the plane creaks like an old church pew as we climb.

My seatmate is as friendly as everyone else on the plane, and has just moved to Nashville from Phoenix. He tells me real estate in the city is expensive and the food is good—he seems almost like he moved there to eat.

It is a weird time for me to be on a plane for work. After the climate report from the UN, each flight now seems differently dangerous. And yet I know the biggest problems are not in plain sight and are bigger than my travel habits—cargo shipping alone is one of the worst polluters, as is meat, and we're already in the place where the Greenland ice sheet is melting, and the methane at the North Pole is burping up in gulps, as land meant to stay frozen goes soft in the heat. Bold scientists fill my Twitter feed, talking about the need for solutions for these transformations, while the Trump administration claims it doesn't know who drew up the report.

I walk to the back of the plane for coffee, passing the bridal cheer squad, who are busy with their myriad devices, streaming videos, their hair shoulder length and gleaming, like sisters, all of them busily posting selfies from the flight, determinedly excited. Can we get a cheer squad for the change to come, a sequel to *Bring It On* called *Keep It in the Ground*?

We touch down. My driver is in a pink taxi called the Love Taxi; he's a disgruntled man who's angry that people walk with their phones. He doesn't want to wear a seat belt. The car's lonely pinging stops when he at last gives in. The earth needs a sound like that, I think, and then I pass the TV screens in my hotel lobby, all footage of the hurricanes.

Until next time, I remain,

ALEXANDER CHEE
BRADFORD, VERMONT

DEAR McSWEENEY'S,
It's been a long time since we've sent you an update. Here's an update: there are only more reasons to stay home than there were last time we spoke. Melting ice caps, hurricanes, sharks, purple drank: who would brave it? It's not safe, especially now that we have dependents (Jenny's two children;

Peter's incontinent cat, Hubbell). To venture outside is to risk grave injury. Just this past year, Peter almost lost his foot to a pseudomonas infection he caught wading in the Anacostia River, and Jenny got a pretty bad sunburn while doing water aerobics. When it rains, we guess, it pours.

It occurs to us that all our current complaints are problems of liquidity: the incontinence, the hurricanes, the Lean, the pool, and the waterborne infection. But maybe it's better to say that these dilemmas are fluid. We don't know if they'll get better or worse. We know only that they'll keep changing. You can't step in the same river twice. As Peter could tell you, you probably shouldn't step in the river at all.

But enough about us. McSweeney's is turning twenty. We remember what we were like when we were twenty-something shut-in detectives, and we write to urge you not to make the same mistakes we did. Stop pretending you like Pavement and admit that the band you actually like is Ace of Base. SnackWell's Devil's Food Cookie Cakes will make you fat. Buy a lot of L'Oreal Studio Line Gelling Curls because it's the only thing that controls your frizz and at some point they're going to discontinue it. Don't use Fruitopia as a mixer. In May 1996, when you meet your sister for dinner at Chili's, don't order the chicken Caesar; it's gone off. Don't waste any more time wondering where your knockoff Ray-Bans are. They fell behind the dresser, but you won't find them until you move out.

We're probably wasting our breath. We know you won't listen, just like our young charges ignore us when we implore them not to leave things where they don't belong. Like Peter says to Hubbell, "That's not a litter box," and now look at the mess we're in.

So here we are. Still, it's not all bad. Our dependents make pleasant company and have nice hair, making us think they got some of the better recessive genes. The world remains full of compelling mysteries, now solved by others via extremely enter-taining podcasts and subreddits. In the meantime, we continue to turn our attentions to the abandoned Popsicle melting on the upholstered ottoman; the puddle next to, but not in, the cat box; and the shark docu-mentary, while we wait for the next generation to save us.

Yours,

JENNY TRAIG & PETER McGRATH, SHUT-IN DETECTIVES
ANN ARBOR, MICHIGAN, AND SILVER SPRING, MARYLAND

DEAR McSWEENEY'S,

Please, for the love of God and/or Terry Gross, can we all agree to just stop making podcasts? Ira Glass, this is mainly your fault. Damn you and your perfect male vocal fry. Well, it's your fault, yes, but also the fault of the big money and/or venture capitalists that turned you from a Chicago wonk into a Chelsea "creative," like, actually, with the divorce and the condo board disputes and all.

Podcasts, we all know, are *in*. Your dead grandma (read: my dead grandma) listened to the radio. Now we're all streaming "on-demand audio content" straight to our Apple or Android (LOL) device. Yes, for my own hipster cred, I used to listen to *This American Life* (*TAL*, for those in the know) back when it was on the radio.

When I'm on a road trip, I love to listen to the radio, and I love public radio shows like *TAL* and *Selected Shorts*, live readings of short stories. I have a vivid memory of taking a trip with my first girlfriend just after we broke up. We were trying to rebuild our relationship as a friendship. I was driving us back from Vermont, where we had camped and had absolutely not slept together, not even once. On *Selected Shorts*, we heard Aasif Mandvi read a story by Jhumpa Lahiri. It's a story of the silences that haunt a relationship, and the pain and joy of filling those silences together.

We started to get out of the range of the radio station just as the story was ramping up to its conclusion. I looked at her, my ex-girlfriend, and she looked at me. We knew each other better than any other people knew either of us. I pulled the car over to the side of the freeway so we could listen, together, to the story's end, even as the radio hissed and popped static. We would lose the station only a minute or two farther down the road. I held her hand as we sat, cars zooming past us, and listened. The wake of each car, moving at seventy miles an hour, gently rocked our car, a small force, but one I could feel. I cried. "They wept together, for the things they now knew," the story ends. My ex and I sat in silence, other than from the radio. She didn't cry with me.

Hi, that's my "radio voice," and this has been an excerpt from my new narrative podcast, Yes, I Am a Male Bisexual, Look at Me Existing, *now available from WNYC on Apple Podcasts or wherever podcasts can be found.*

So, you see, it's not that I don't love radio.

It's just that I don't really love podcasts enough, apparently, for the world we're living in now. And, look, I hate to say this, but I *really* don't love bad podcasts, and, OMG, so many of them are really just pretty bad.

All of this, like everything else in 2018, is entirely to do with money and technology.

Money first. About those venture capitalists. There has been a huge shift in how we listen to things. Podcasts are basically radio on demand, and they're Netflixing the audio world. Ads work well in this type of content, and there are entire podcasting companies that just fired their podcast-making staff to focus exclusively on making podcast software. The software they make lets you drop in different ads through the lifetime of a radio show so you don't have to upload a new audio file and lose the public record of the five hundred thousand suckers who listened to your Squarespace ads while trapped on the 405. The 405 is an LA thing, right? So anyway, you get money for the initial ads, and then *more* money for up-to-date ads later.

This letter to the editor is brought to you by Squarespace. Today in our Midroll, a game! You have to guess which of these websites Joe has actually registered using Squarespace! Are you ready: messybottom .com or cryinginyourworkbathroomstall .com. Trick question, tricks: he owns both of them. Use your special McSweeney's promo code—lolsob—now for 15 percent off your first website or domain name.

And, while there's basically no data anywhere to back any of this up, it seems as though ads get a better return on investment when they're read into your earbuds by someone you actually like. And podcasts feel intimate; listeners tend to actually like the hosts of their favorite shows. I made my website from Squarespace after hearing an ad on *TAL*, and I even got 10 percent off! Ira would never steer me wrong. So it doesn't matter if venture capitalists like podcasts; they love podcast ads. JK, venture capitalists aren't capable of love, duh, but they make up for it with their yachts in their Saint-Tropezes.

This letter to the editor is brought to you by Casper mattresses, OMG, they're so soft, I personally own, like, four of them.

I don't care if you've embraced the word *pod* like the *Pod Save America* guys, or hate it with a passion, like everyone else. (Seriously, podcast world, get better beefs. Like, maybe be mad that basically everyone is, like, straight and white and mostly boring.) What we know for sure is this: podcasts are making a small number of people very, very rich.

Just like everything else in 2018.

That's the thing: advertisers want to reach millions, not dozens. They aren't paying anyone who makes a show without a huge audience. It's hard even to sell ads for shows with tens of thousands of listeners, like the one I do. But it's hard to make a show *by* and *for* queer people, just for example, that manages to reach millions.

Mail K... ch... chimp.

The rest of us are just trying to get into that little crowd. Which is where the technological barrier to entry comes in. Unlike, you know, a TV show, which requires cameras and boom microphones and big, fancy computers for editing, podcasts need only a microphone. It's hard to make a TV show look professional. Any idiot can turn on a mic and talk.

And, oh lord, have they ever.

It's true that podcasts are pretty democratic. For not a lot of money, you can make one, and get it on iTunes and everything. Except, without the right connections, the fact that you're on iTunes will be the most remarkable thing about your show. I read somewhere that there are an absolute metric fuckton (I'm a scientist; that's a scientific term) of podcasts, and that the median number of listens per episode is something like fifty.

And then you had season one of *Serial*, which broke the internet and made Sarah Koenig a household

name. Even Kim Kardashian listened, and so what if that was four years later? Season one of *Serial* made Mailchimp and Squarespace household names too.

But, hey, everyone, this doesn't feel sustainable. This feels just like everything that's wrong with everything else. People who have been doing this forever are making more podcasts, and they mostly sound the same, and everyone's listening, and they're getting rich. The rest of us are making podcasts that basically no one is listening to, not even our friends, not even our mothers.

So. Look. Can this be, like, a suicide pact, a Devil's Triangle? I'll stop making mine, you'll stop making yours, and Ira Glass can finally go on vacation? Terry Gross can stay on the radio, but, like, just take a hiatus from Apple Podcasts (or wherever you download audio content)?

Can we all just, like, cool off for a little while, fuck over the venture capitalists, and then come back and decide not to fuck with Apple, either, and just, like, not care who has a banner ad for Pride Month? Can we just all try to go a little more slowly, make shows that are actually worth listening to, made by, and for, an actually diverse community of people? Can we please, please do that? Can we all just please, for now, not make any more podcasts, not any at all, none? A radio silence that we can fill with our own stories, for now, sharing our own stories with our lovers, past and present, speaking into the silences we too often, now, try to fill with making, and listening to, static.

Sincerely yours, a scientist, writer, and podcast host,

JOSEPH OSMUNDSON
NEW YORK, NEW YORK

P.S. Next week on *Yes, I Am a Male Bisexual, Look at Me Existing*, there will be three acts of stories about me totally existing. Don't forget to subscribe and rate us five stars on iTunes.

DEAR McSWEENEY'S,

I've been meaning to write you, I swear. Life's been moving so fast lately, it almost feels like it's been running—traveling, teaching, reading student work, trying to balance it all. I just got back to Iowa City from New York City. I was there for a photo shoot with *T Magazine*— the style magazine of the *New York Times*. There's an article coming out about black male novelists, poets, essayists, and playwrights, and I've been selected to be included in the cohort. What an honor, huh? The film director Boots Riley came up with the concept for the photo shoot, and they got as many of us together as possible and snapped the shot. We're surrounded by books like hoarders, and we're all elevated, rising up out of the stacks. The group picture was taken in the library at the Brooklyn Historical Society, but we spent the majority of the day getting ready inside the sanctuary of a large church.

I've been trying to slow down the pace of life, but it seems that a hectic summer turned into a hectic fall, and I'm starting to settle with the idea that fast and hectic may be the state of affairs for a while. With the way things have been going, I don't believe in coincidences anymore. Instead, I've begun to trust that everything is happening as it's supposed to. I was supposed to be in South Africa—right now!—at a writing conference, but it just wasn't in the cards. Fate had other plans for me. The day after the trip was canceled, I got word that the black male writer photo shoot was being scheduled for the day I would've been scheduled to leave for South Africa.

It was an unforgettable day. There was an incredible amount of laughter, bonding, and camaraderie as we all milled around, waiting for everyone to be processed through hair, makeup, and wardrobe. The *T Magazine* piece isn't out yet as I write this, not sure how much I'm really supposed to be talking about it, but I figure you can keep a secret, right? It was a meeting of the generations. The OGs got introduced to us young bucks, truly a special occasion, nothing short of inspiring. The closest correlative experience from my own life takes me back to my basketball-playing days. I remember the first time I played in a gym with elite and distinguished athletes—NBA, Division I, and guys who play overseas, the sort of crowd where everyone has a name and a reputation. Never before in my life had I been in the presence of thirty other black male writers who are actively publishing.

James McBride was there, and he held court in the best way, dropping gems like a jewel thief as he politicked with us. Even he could feel the energy in the room. "We'll never be together in this configuration again," he said. When I saw him walk in, it felt like something had come full circle. First of all, the brother was too fresh! He strolled in wearing a nice gray suit and top hat, and two different-colored Adidas shell-toes, white with black stripes and black with white stripes. (Our directions were to wear black dress shoes.) Being from Boston, I'm partial to Adidas, but the outfit was smooth, and seeing him shot me back to a time. This photoshoot was the second time we'd met. I jogged his memory about our first meeting.

I was a sophomore at Susquehanna University back in January of 2008, and James McBride and his band came to campus for Martin Luther King Jr. Day to put on a concert and for James to deliver the keynote address at winter convocation. I remember my roommate and I had gotten into it about something. What, I'm not sure, but I remember going to hear Mr. McBride's speech—I'd recently read *The Color of Water: A Black Man's Tribute to His White Mother*—and was feeling inspired. The overall message of his talk was to "do what you love until they pay you for it," or something to that effect. Fast-forward to after the assembly. Let's just say I temporarily "liberated" my roommate's Lexus to scorch some recreational "flowers" on the back roads. As I drove back to campus, airing out the car, I see James McBride walking on the side of the road. If you've ever been to central Pennsylvania, then you already know it's intensely racist, no place for a black man to be walking around looking lost. I pulled over and offered him a ride, which he accepted. He smelled the flowers I'd been burning, and asked me what I did on campus besides burn the flowers. I told him I was a creative-writing major and his eyebrows arched as he looked at me. He asked what I was reading at the time, and, still being under the magic of the flowers, I remember blanking, and him telling me that I'd need to read a whole lot if I really wanted to do this. I remember him encouraging me, saying that he hoped one day I'd put a book in the world and that we'd cross paths again.

I have now put a book in the world. He didn't remember our first meeting as vividly as I did, but he was just as warm, welcoming, and approachable as I'd remembered (though a lot more medaled than he was back then). I suppose both of us have grown. In the church, I explained an old fear I'd had about dying broke and in obscurity that I developed after reading how things were at the end for Zora Neale Hurston, one of my favorite authors. He said, "We're all going to die in relative obscurity, anyway." Now, at first I wasn't sure what he was getting at, but he continued with something like "No one remembers the third song on Luther Vandross's second album, but people still study Miles Davis's *Kind of Blue*. Who do

you think made more money? It's not about attention. It's about if it will last. The musicians like Miles Davis, Bird, Dizzy, Cannonball Adderley— those guys weren't paid right, but it's the jazz the people remember. Writing these novels and telling these stories—that's the jazz." He explained the ultimate purpose we ought to keep in mind: leaving good books behind, as seeds and blueprints for the young brothers who've not yet arrived.

As I walked away from the photo shoot and back to the hotel with a few young fellow writers, I felt energized.

I'm really eager for this *T Magazine* piece to come out. With the madness that is our political climate at the moment, it's very important for this group photo to exist in the world. Black men are represented by so many negative images, and for the sake of balance the world needs to see some of the other side of the spectrum: a group of black men surrounded by books, committing no crimes but instead being celebrated for black excellence, engaging in the effort of furthering the culture and conversation, bushwhacking for the brothers coming up behind us. It's important.

Hugs and hand pounds,

MARCUS BURKE
IOWA CITY, IOWA

MONONA

BY RAVEN LEILANI

IT BEGAN WHEN A new breed of amphibious butterfly migrated to Wisconsin's Lake Monona. The butterflies had the iridescent blue of the Karner and the thick veins of the monarch. The lake's fresh water was sweeter than even the state violet's pistil, and so, without anything to feast upon them, the fields from which the butterflies came grew swollen, and crept up around the houses in the county like soft lilac wisteria. Before, the town had been spare and nondescript. There was an old Lutheran church that had once been a textile mill, and the walls were still spongy from the steam. There was a strip mall with a nail parlor and an ammo shop. And there was a single Thai restaurant owned by descendants of Wisconsin's first Vikings, which was apparent in the quality of the pad see ew. The butterflies came one at a time, and then in pairs.

They were welcome, photogenic interlopers. Brides blushed at the altar as butterflies alighted on their veils. Then more came, and the town watched as the butterflies thickened the lake. Children didn't want to take baths or sleep, and Minnesota was building a wall on its border. The butterflies did not discriminate. Any wet place was good. A lake, a throat.

A year after the first fumigation attempt, Lee went on a second date with Jon, a part-time fisherman. Their first date had been unremarkable. She'd chewed her fingernails during a matinee, and he'd rolled up his pant leg to show her an old football injury. The second date began more earnestly. He brought her a wreath made of violets, even though the town was covered in them. He was a man who thought ordinary things were beautiful, and she assumed this was why he'd been drawn to her. On Tuesdays he went diving into the lake to catch any salmon that were still alive under the silver layer of butterflies. He sold them to the locals for double what the normal asking price had been before the infestation, and they paid it.

When she arrived at his house, he placed the wreath on her head and took a long, pink salmon from a cooler full of ice. He put the fish into her hands, and she trembled at the breath she still felt in it. She feigned indifference, hyperaware of the gills fanning against her palms. He slunk across his kitchen, retrieved a knife, and motioned for her to put the fish on the counter. She tried to think of something to say. She thought of his slim body, a dagger pushing through layers of thirsty butterflies. She thought of the departed six-year-old Erica Hudson, and eighty-five-year-old Garrett Kinnison, two mouths falling slack mid-slumber, the butterflies seeking their throats. She adjusted the wreath atop her head, and watched as he pushed the blade down with the heel of his hand.

The scales peeled away from the fish like sequins. In her mind, hunting for her own food was romantic, but turned outward onto a cutting board, the fish soured her stomach. She looked around and found a perfect source of distraction in the chaos of his apartment. It was covered in a patchwork of ash, empty bottles, and other detritus, the walls inexplicably lined with an extensive collection of women's shoes. She struggled not to bite her fingernails in front of him, but she was nervous. After the infestation, the fish in the lake had become illegal to catch, eat, or sell. She noticed a pair of blue stilettos stuck between the cushions of his couch.

He cupped the guts in his hands and tossed them into the trash. She felt her appetite returning. As he washed his hands, she noticed that he wore a plain gold ring on his left hand. She didn't know if it was new or if this detail had simply slipped her attention. He sighed and put his hands on his hips, said he was going to take a shower and that she was welcome to join. He had a crooked smile, and every time he showed his teeth, she took great pleasure in the conspicuousness of his incisors. And then he was wrapping the fish in white paper and tossing it into a mini freezer full of ice, leading her with his long fingers to a tiny bathroom with turquoise tiles and a single dirty mirror. He was out of his clothes, and she barely had time to register the length of his body, his bare feet, the ruddy wisps of chest and armpit hair, his eyes, deep and Byzantine, as he drew her into the shower, and when had she undressed? And then she was washing her face with his plain, single-male lye bar soap, taking pleasure in the sudden nakedness of her face. And then he was moving inside her, and she wanted to look into his eyes, but he kept them closed, and she noticed that his eyelids, once drawn down completely, were almost iridescent in the poor bathroom light, almost silver.

Once toweled off and dressed, they proceeded back into the kitchen in a very businesslike fashion. He brought out a clove of garlic, sesame oil, and ginger. Wordlessly, he whisked them together, seeming more serious than she had ever seen him. She wanted to make a joke, finding it absurd that even after they'd made love, there was still ice to break. The truth was, she didn't know if they had anything in common. They'd gone to high school together. She'd wanted to leave Dane County ever since she could dream, but she had come back defeated after five short years of flailing in a city over a hundred miles away. Then she'd seen him in the supermarket palming onions, and remembered the very particular way Wisconsin boys could be beautiful.

She'd had a persistent crush on him for three years of high school, and suspected that no matter who he was now, the remnants of that old, warm feeling obstructed her vision of him. It didn't matter. He proffered his fingers for taste-testing, and without a word she leaned forward and sucked them. It was interesting, though, that this, too, was very procedural, and when he asked what she thought of the taste, she knew he meant only that. As he took his hand away, she noticed that between the fingers of his left hand was that same iridescent color that lined his eyelids.

When he plated the food, there was a slight tremor in his fingers. She looked on, wondering if he gave much thought to the illegality of his enterprise. Even though there was nothing apparently radical about him, he seemed to be one of those men who did not give much consideration to the law, not out of self-righteousness but out of a certain lackadaisy that rendered him bright, loose. When he asked her to take a seat in the living room, she did so, suspecting that he could feel her hovering and needed some space.

She pulled the pair of shoes from the couch cushions and set them aside. She tried not to think anything of it. Yet there was the box of sanitary napkins under the sink in the bathroom, the lipstick in the medicine cabinet. She looked to the door, suddenly anxious that he had a wife who might come in tired from work to find another woman moving her things, eating her food, sucking her husband's fingers.

He set the table and beckoned her over. When she sat down, she realized her dress was inside out. She crossed her arms over herself as he came over with the plates. The food was arranged so deliberately that for a moment she couldn't bring herself to start eating. She pretended to be busy with her napkin. This pretentious part of his character, so dissonant with the rest of him, made her curious. He pulled a bottle of wine from thin air. He poured a high glass for her, and only a little for himself. When she began to eat, she could feel his eyes watching closely for a reaction. She closed her eyes. It was a sensation beyond her tongue.

"What makes it taste like this?" she asked.

"Butter, salt," he answered, but she knew he understood what she meant. She knew he'd heard the rumors around town, about the fish, about him. People bought his fish, but found the secrecy of the transaction distasteful. They paid him in cash and retreated to their homes, where they dined and wondered how a boy who had been so well liked had become so strange. She took another bite and indulged in the sensation, the warm, anesthetic thrum. It compelled her to close her eyes again, and when she opened them, it was to take another sip of wine.

"The way I feel. Is this why the fish are illegal? The butterflies are doing something to them?"

"Why? Are you scared?"

"A little. I've never broken the law," she replied, and he put his hand down gently over her hand, told her to take her time. Maybe she should've resented his presumption, his ego. She was a little embarrassed by his fervor, by her easy compliance. Still, she ate the rest of her meal in the same languorous fashion, too engrossed in how it made her feel to be bothered by his watchful gaze.

When he took their plates away, she exhaled. She felt a little dizzy and considered that she hadn't known him long enough to discern whether or not he was a terrible man, and whether he was, in fact, capable of slipping her pills. To abolish the thought, she got to her feet, trying to gauge the weight of her legs. After a few moments of walking around the living room while he did the dishes, she felt only the delirium of too much wine. The blue stilettos caught her eye again, and she went over and picked them up.

"My favorite," he said from behind her, and she turned, unaware that he'd been watching. He asked her to sit down. He was smoking a short cigarette that he'd worn tucked behind his ear during dinner. He knelt in front of her and held up one of the shoes. "I really love this pair." A cloud of smoke obscured his face. "Can I put them on you?" She nodded, and when the first shoe went on easily, he seemed almost relieved.

"Who do these belong to?" she finally asked, as he put on the second one.

"My wife," he answered, and then was quick to amend this. "My ex-wife." She felt the air in the room thin.

"You're divorced."

"I'm sorry I didn't phrase that better. I mean, she died." She couldn't move herself to ask how, seeing the look in his eye, feeling an ugly impulse in herself to wonder if she now had to contend with a woman martyred. Though they continued on to less-somber topics during the rest of the evening, she couldn't shake the feeling that there was something else breathing in the house, a thing she couldn't find anywhere in a physical picture, manifested only in a suite of designer shoes. And so at the end of the night, when he asked her to take the shoes and wear them on their next date, she said yes.

In the week before their next date, the town was embroiled in a small scandal involving two teenagers who'd jumped from the roof of an office building in an eastern part of the county. There was a brief segment about it on the news. The camera zoomed in on the lake, and a reporter held up a litmus stick. She said the lake was growing increasingly alkaline, and that after this most recent incident, there would be a town hall. She said parents wanted the person responsible to be held accountable. In the next shot, one of the mothers of the deceased raked a hand through her hair and said: Everyone knows it's him.

Lee scoured the internet for information about Jon's departed wife. She checked the local paper online, brushing past the news of what minor ecosystems had been disturbed in the wake of the butterfly infestation to comb through old obituaries. She found a short, antiseptic snippet about his wife, Melissa. She had been twenty-nine, thin, and owned a storefront in the sticks trading in culinary goods. Lee felt ashamed to be threatened by this, but nevertheless used the information to travel down a number of internet rabbit holes that led her to grainy photos of local awards ceremonies, clips about collegiate extracurriculars, and one high-definition photo of her at an annual fair, looking directly into the camera with still, gray eyes. But the important thing, the reason she'd searched, was the two curt words at the end of the obituary, *apparent suicide.* The night of their third date, she used one of the pictures she'd found to style herself. She arrived at his door, and a hand darted out and pulled her inside. In her high, unfamiliar shoes, she toppled to her knees. The house was dark.

"I need to show you something. Please don't scream," he said, and then he turned on the lights. At first he appeared abstractly, an unbalanced ratio of shadow and limb, and then she saw them, bright and jointed and velveteen—two silver butterfly wings. She got to her feet, and without meaning to started backing toward the door. The air seethed around him, and she tried to look at his face, but found her eyes roving of their own accord, following the veins in his coin-colored wings. From farther away, it was less grotesque, and in a way almost beautiful, though never for more than a few seconds at a time. If she looked too long, she realized the full, magnified texture of them, the capillaries pulsing between layers of silver skin, thin and fetal.

"When did this happen?"

"Thursday." He offered no more information. She had a horrible image of him, half human, half larva. When he moved, she saw how the wings had compromised his balance. His effort to remain upright was conspicuous, and she turned away. He chose a long coat to obscure the bottoms of the wings, which were edged in iridescent green. He got his keys, grabbed their picnic basket, and slunk through the door. He locked it, told her there was a chance of rain. But rain meant nothing, to be wearing a dead woman's shoes meant nothing, when she looked into his eyes and saw that he wasn't acknowledging something terrible.

The town was still purple and swollen. It had been a week since another out-of-state agency had sprayed where the concentration of butterflies was highest, a week since they'd failed. When he took her hand, she realized that it was trembling, that he still wore his ring. By the time they were halfway to the park, night was rising out of dusk. He brought out two cigarettes and handed her one, and she didn't realize how much she needed it until she was breathing in.

"Do you ever think about how much is out of our control?" he asked suddenly.

"All the time," she answered, because this had been her mantra for the six full months she'd spent collecting herself at her parents' house after failing to live on her own. But when she looked at him, she wondered if he was thinking of his wife, his new form.

"I miss high school. I was in control of everything." Because she'd known him then, she knew it wasn't hyperbole. He had been an affable jock, a middle-of-the-road lineman with surprising teeth. The surprise was that they were bad, but he was so tender you forgot it until the next time he smiled. He could easily have abused his popularity, and in some cases he did—people did his homework, and he basked in the attention of the moony and weird—but mostly he was careless, every arm of his life suffused with ease.

"I don't." She thought of her own set of hallways, the loneliness. Even now, there was still some small part of her always needing to prove she was wanted.

"Which high school did you go to?"

"We went to high school together. Same grade," she replied, and he scratched his head. His embarrassment at this amplified hers.

"I'm sorry. I bet you were the smartest girl there." From this she could tell that he now understood they belonged to different phyla.

"I thought I was."

They settled down between two trees, smoothed out a bedsheet on the grass. He lit a couple of candles and started unpacking the picnic basket. With a bit of horror, she realized he'd prepared sushi. She paused, thought of the wings furled beneath his long jacket, and wondered how he still expected her to eat anything from the lake. And yet she was distracted by the ceremony with which he set out the spread, his reverence for presentation apparent in each lavish roll, the careful geometry of seaweed, rice, and roe, the shred of sashimi, the fat, glutinous rolls spliced with the odd vegetable or fruit.

"I like your hair tonight," he said, uncorking a bottle of ice wine. Again, she felt something between them, sucking up the air. They sat for a while in silence. She watched him eat, surprised to find his indulgent manner unchanged. He still took long moments to savor the taste; he still closed his eyes and leaned into it. She took up her chopsticks and pretended to dine. Of course, he noticed. Before, it hadn't been so irritating when he'd watched her eat. It had been a little thrilling, sort of sweet that he was so invested. But now, when there was no conversation to buffer her efforts to consume as little as possible, his attention put her on edge.

"You still wear your ring." He looked up from his plate, and immediately she was sorry to have blurted it out. Yet now, in hindsight, when she considered his ring, and the shoes on her feet, the interior of his home seemed shrine-like, stricken with unacknowledged grief.

"Old habits." He didn't elaborate. She thought of him groggy and half awake, turning in bed to discover his new, fluttering appendages. "She was smart, like you, and so it still doesn't make any sense." Cruelly, even though she'd never known his wife, she resented the presumption that their intellects were comparable. Even as she knew when he said *smart*, it was a blanket term that sometimes doubles as *square.*

"What doesn't make any sense?"

"Nothing was wrong," he said, and because of his transformation, because of the unspoken contract to say nothing more about it, she doubted his ability to admit if, in fact, something had been wrong. "And I kept telling her to stop listening to what the town was saying. This infestation has made everyone so weird."

"What happened?" She felt a little like a fraud, inquiring when she already knew, but she was curious to see what he would say.

"She jumped from the roof of our house and broke her neck," he said so bluntly that she stilled. She considered the image of a woman in her work clothes, climbing upward through the creeping violets, a completely innocuous thing, until it wasn't.

"She wasn't depressed?"

"No, I told you." She got the feeling that this was a question he was tired of answering. "It was the town. The town killed her."

"I don't understand," she said, and he leaned forward, his face malformed by candlelight.

"I know you've heard the rumors. About the fish giving people the ability to fly?" he said, and she stared, feeling awkward in his apparent denial. "We fought about it a lot. She thought I was being stubborn, and I thought she was going mad. But what would I look like, believing in magic?" She thought of the teenage suicides. She thought perhaps this particular rumor wasn't true, but no doubt it helped his business. He had to know this. He had to know that he was feeding this facet of the town's paranoia. Again, she thought of the interior of his house, and wondered if it was not only grief, but guilt.

"I guess it's not always black and white," she said, not wanting to press the subject of his wife any further.

"It's as black and white as this: my wife thought she could fly, and she couldn't."

He walked her home in silence. After the contentious dinner, she hadn't planned on asking him inside, but as he stood on her doorstep and she gazed again into his eyes, she felt her resolve crumble. Perhaps it was her own lurid curiosity, the specter of his wife hanging in the air between them, the memory of their fusion. But as she drew him inside, she knew it was the fear. It was the fear that made it exciting. It was fear making his eyes wild, shucking his coat from his shoulders in the dark, trembling his wings as they drew outward, trembling his hands as they reached for hers, fear in the streetlamp light slivering his body into white and silver clips, in the shoes she slung into another room so she wouldn't have to think about their owner, in whatever protein continued to fold him out of human form, in the realization that she wasn't smart or disciplined enough to combat the machinations of her id, which made her arrogant enough to leave a place exactly as mundane as she deserved, fear in the failure all around them, reanimated as a pair of empty shoes and a pair of bodies using each other to cope. And so a few days later, when the fog of the night had cleared, she shouldn't have been surprised to find that the town, itself filled with fear, had finally found an appropriate target.

* * *

It was a Tuesday, perfect fishing weather. His routine was already a badly kept secret, something people muttered about behind closed doors while unwrapping the white paper from their contraband. She was still savoring the remnants of the night they'd shared as she made her way over to visit him. She stopped at the sight of a crowd standing around his house. She waded through the crowd until she came to stand before his door, which was ajar, almost torn off its hinges.

A policeman emerged from the house with a fist of fishing line; another emerged with Jon's tackle box, an innocuous little kit covered with stickers for local beer gardens. She knew then that his secret was no longer a secret. She looked again at the tackle box and felt her heart sinking. It wasn't rational. She knew on some level that what he was doing was reckless, that something needed to be done. But it was another thing entirely to see it happening, to see the inside of his house from the outside, the terrible claustrophobia of it bracketed by a broken door.

Then a gasp moved through the crowd, and she looked up. And perhaps it was the daylight that rendered the sight even more improbable, or the schadenfreude of the growing crowd, but she felt her stomach turn. She watched two police officers carry a gurney through the crowd, a white bedsheet tossed haphazardly over the body. Even from what little she could see, she could tell his body had continued to change in the days they'd been apart. The form she saw now was barely human, but that wasn't the detail she would remember when she went to bed, when she woke up and drove to work listening to the morning news. She would think how funny it was to hear the words *mutation* and *poison* on the radio in reference to a gentle, reckless man; how funny it was to hear a local scientist weigh in on what had happened, when everyone already knew well enough that they did not have the words to describe it. What she would remember was the police emerging from his house, the silver wing wilting around a standard-issue bullet.

MOURNERS

BY SHRUTI SWAMY

"YOU HAVEN'T EATEN ANYTHING," Reggie says. They can hear Maya
with the baby in the other room: the baby is crying, then being hushed.

"I'm not hungry," says Mark.

"How now, gentle cuz?" Reggie says. She puts her hand on his rough
cheek. Her face is sardonic as always, but there is kindness in it. Then
Maya comes in with the baby, whose little cheeks are wet with tears.
Seeing her father, the baby reaches her small hands out to him. Maya is
wearing a sleeveless dress. Her eyes, thickly lidded, normally languid,
are now red and tired.

"Will you hold her?" says Maya.

"No," says Mark.

Maya looks at Reggie, who opens her arms.

When she learned Chariya had died, Maya immediately left her small apartment. It was windy in New York; she wore a coat and gloves and a scarf and a hat. Daylight passed. She walked by men and women and looked at them with just her face exposed. But from this small expanse of skin they could read her perfectly. Her mind was stunned, her body hungry, a hunger that frightened her. She slept in her seat with a hand over her mouth while her body flew west: she was dreaming of being fucked. It was Reggie who came to get her at the airport, looking rough in the unfussy clothes of a farmwife, holding Chariya's baby in a carrier. Standing under the ARRIVALS sign, Maya pressed tears back into her eyes with the heels of her hands.

Maya sits in the bathtub for a long time before she turns on the tap. It was Chariya's room, her sea room, where she had taken long baths, and where she had given birth. Blue tiles, blue walls, blue towels, and a flat, gray light coming in through the window. With her foot, she nudges open the tap, which floods heat. She looks at her body, wavering under the water. What use is a body? There is no milk in her breasts.

"Maya." Mark's voice. It comes from far away, and she lifts her head above the translucent surface and closes the tap. Then the house becomes silent. He says again, "Maya."

"What?"

"I—I left something in there."

"What."

"My reading glasses. Do you see them?"

"No." Still she can feel him standing, pressed against the closed door. She says, "I found seven white hairs today."

"Where?"

"At my left temple."

"You're young still."

"Chariya is going gray."

"Was." From far away they can hear Reggie with the baby, cooing, the sound an animal makes. The sound of the baby's laughter. She has been fussy, getting her teeth in. But the last few days she has sensed the change in the house and has become quiet.

"Maya."

"No," she says.

Five or six, dusk gathers quietly outside until the room is filled with it. White moths spread their wings against the windows, but from the inside they are just their shapes: black. When the baby cries, Maya takes her and rocks her against her body. Soon the baby is sleeping. Maya and Reggie begin to talk about Chariya. From the other room, Mark listens to the fall of their voices. They are tender as they speak about Chariya.

"She'd just cut her hair. Did you see it?"

"No," says Maya.

"Short as a man's. Like a French girl's. It suited her."

"People used to think we were twins. But she was older."

"Couldn't have been by much."

"Five years."

"Five? I don't believe it. I thought Irish twins at least."

Mark thinks of the sisters together. They both stand at the edge of the lake. Chariya is not yet pregnant. One wades in and the other stays on the shore: one dark, the other darker. Then they are each other's reflection. It is Chariya who floats up, arms and hair spread out, in the green water. She is wearing a blue bathing suit that makes the skin of her inner arms and thighs seem golden. When she wants to, she can look sublime, so happy.

From somewhere he can hear Chariya laughing, and his heart leaps up. But then he realizes it is Maya. Maya, as she begins to hum a song to the sleeping child, a lullaby that Chariya sang too. A lullaby for his daughter, but he accepts it as his. And sleeps.

The women are in the kitchen in the morning when Mark wakes. Reggie's hair is wet, and Maya sits very quietly at the table, with the baby again in her arms. The baby examines a small apple that Reggie has given her. She doesn't yet have the teeth to bite it. She keeps bringing it to her mouth. "Are you hungry?" says Reggie. She gives him a cup of coffee.

"Yes," he says. Maya has dressed herself in a yellow sweater that was once Chariya's, and a soft blue skirt. Reggie is in jeans.

"You were sleeping so deeply we thought you were dead," says Maya.

Mark sits down at the table, facing Maya. Her bottom teeth are crooked. She has never had braces, like her older sister did.

"Don't look at me like that."

"You've got a real wasp problem," says Reggie. She points to the window.

"I thought I got them all."

"Well, you didn't."

"The cold will get them."

"The cold won't do anything. I'll call someone." Reggie is examining his face. He sees himself sitting barefoot in his shorts in his kitchen with these women, and feels ridiculous.

"No, I'll do it," he says. "I'll do it."

It is a task for later, for dusk. Reggie makes eggs. They sit at the table to eat. The baby has set down the apple and is pulling unhappily at her ear. She wears an austere white jumper, and with her dark cap of hair looks like a tiny monk. Mark saw a child's skull once, in a medical museum, with all the adult teeth poised under the milk. The skull he saw was from an older child, four or five years old. But Mark sees there the skull of his daughter. Quiet bone, and growing, the teeth expanding, creaking like swollen wood as they push outward, slicing the gums. The double grin that lasts into death, while the eyes and nose and ears fall away, become dark holes. He lifts his eyes to Maya, whose chin rests on the baby's head. As she turns her face to glance out the window, he catches his breath. For a simple, brilliant moment, she is Chariya, the cocoa-brown curve of jaw, her fierce eyes with their curly lashes. He stays very still and looks at her.

"Stop it," she says, feeling him, facing him, and starts to cry. "Can you please stop it?"

Will it rain? Rain trembles in the clouds, but the clouds never break. Mark is tired, Maya is tired, Reggie is tired, tireless. She is mending a burst seam of a coat, Chariya's. Reggie squinting in the lamplight to thread the needle. Why bother?

But she must bother. She has seen Chariya wear the coat again and again. It is the seam that holds the chest to the arm, under the left armpit, her waving arm. Chariya stands at the gate and waves, the sweater underneath showing yellow at the opening. Chariya's dark face at the gate as Reggie reverses the car and backs down the drive. And Reggie calls, "Careful, you'll tear the whole sleeve off." But Chariya had no time to fix her coat—why else would she cut her hair so short? Chariya had no time to comb her hair. Chariya had no time to read a book she loved. Chariya had no time to go to Paris. Chariya had no time to take a nap.

The house is old and shifts on its haunches, settling. Reggie is not startled by the house's noises. She lives just down the road in an old house of her own, but has slept here since death came. Not slept, but lain unsleeping in the room between her cousin's and the baby's, alert always for the mewling cries of the child as she, hungry, wakes, and alert for Mark's moans as he sleeps—never words, only snuffles and grunts. She can see in his waking eyes the dazed confusion of a very young child. His cheeks are dry and sallow as old paper, the same cheeks upon which she had kissed her blessings on his wedding day, just as she'd kissed blessings upon the soft cheeks of his bride.

Reggie drags the thread through the fabric. She is doing her work by touch, not sight, following the fabric's curve by instinct. What a violence mending does, the needle piercing and piercing. It is a good coat, a fine coat, which held Chariya's body for years, even when the belly was swollen with baby and the button could not reach its hole. Finished, she breaks the thread with her teeth and drapes the coat around her own shoulders.

When evening comes, Mark ties a scarf around his mouth and takes out the poison he had bought for last time. The sky is beautiful, hanging very low down, thick with clouds, and all the trees darken into large shapes in the yard, the apple and lemon trees and the oak. He follows the channel of wasps to its source. Even in the dim light, he can see the nest resting in the space between the roof and the wall of the house. It seems to radiate light, pale as it is, like a moon. You kill the wasps at dusk, after they've finished their day's work and they are returning home. But last time he hadn't been ruthless. The smell of the chemical sickened him. The wasps were soundless, drugged on fumes. They were dizzy and frightened and didn't try to sting. He felt sorry for them and thought he had done enough; he had gone back inside.

Now he watches the last of the wasps fly in. It is fully dark, but his eyes have adjusted. His hands are cold. Before the chemicals coat the nest and dry, a few emerge, flying weirdly, almost drunkenly, then dropping. He sprays and sprays. The rest are trapped in that house of theirs. They die quietly. The bitter smell is all around him, though he tries not to breathe it in.

Mark walks away from the nest and takes a mouthful of evening, gulping it. The air is sweet and cool, and the stars are coming out. It is only six thirty. Inside, they have turned the lights on. The house looks cheerful. He has never stood outside his house, just like this, in the dark, alone, looking in. It feels pleasant and comfortable to be cold outside, looking in like a robber, or a child peering into a neighbor's house. He can see Reggie moving around in the kitchen, but not Maya. He removes the scarf, and the cold air enters his lungs. He can feel it in his chest. For a moment he is awake with it; he has finally woken up. He holds his breath. He is so close to it, to feeling joy, the joy of the body. But it is moving away from him. He cannot reach it. The poison in his hand, the dead are dead. The held breath bursts out of him, and is gone.

Tap, *tap*, *tap*, the fingers of the trees against the window, like the fingers of the dead, asking to be let inside.

The top of a tiny white tooth appears in the baby's lower jaw, like the tip of the moon trying the horizon. It is not centered but set slightly to the right. The baby touches the tooth with her fingers. A familiar taste, almost ugly, the taste of red. At first there is the pure surprise of newness, where there is no fear. But fear comes. She was once soft, all of her soft. Now there is some hardness stuck in her, pushing out from her. She can feel voice building up in her lungs like heat, voice building and building until it spurts from her mouth. Her sound is a comfort around her, the yellow-orange glow she builds. The tooth in the mouth, and where has Mother gone? Mother and not-mother. Mother came when she called, and lifted. Mother tickled and wept. Mother laughed. And Father used to kiss gently but with scratch. Now he doesn't kiss her. She reaches and he turns away. Her voice builds and builds and then a coolness comes into her throat, and she quiets. She bats up her fists and feet and kicks, feeling the limbs working below. There is pure, profound silence at the center. It is courage, the baby. It is the courage to live in an expanding body, with limbs lifting outward, with teeth pushing up, with hands and mind growing finer and more agile, with eyes settling on color, with body unbending from the earth and standing upright, balancing perilously on two legs, and then moving forward, walking, running forward, teeth loosening, filling, knees scraped and healing, voice gaining depth and sureness, hips and breasts accruing, skin darkening, stretching, blood slipping out from the thighs, and death always, always, at the back.

Arms go around, arms lift. When the woman looks at the baby in her arms, the baby looks back at her with her color-shifting eyes, gray now, in the kitchen light. The irises are immense, like a cat's eyes, with hardly any white, the mouth impossibly gentle. She doesn't want to bless the baby, because what good have her blessings done? She moves ice along the hot gums. It clicks against the nub of tooth. They are calm, the woman and the baby. Their silence is mammalian and warm. The woman can smell the milky skin of the baby; the baby can smell the humble soap and hand salve of the woman. It is she, perhaps, who should seek the blessings from this child, who will come to her when she, Reggie, is old, carrying an armful of fragrant lilacs. Placing the lilacs in a vase, as the old woman moves around the kitchen preparing tea. And the old woman draws strength and pleasure, yes, from the fragrant sight of the flowers, but more from the young woman's strong, happy body, the length and gentleness of her limbs, the shine of her dark face.

That night they all eat at the table, they drink wine. It is not good wine but it doesn't matter. They begin to tease each other, and tell jokes, jokes to shock each other into laughter. Laughter tastes funny in their mouths, mixed with the bitter taste of the wine, and then they warm to it. They tell stories of old lovers. Maya rests her bare feet against the legs of her chair. Mark looks at those feet: he would like to become a dog and lick them and the fat bones at her ankle. A lover who wanted to fuck only in the bathrooms of moving trains, a lover who called for his mother as he came, a lover aroused by the sound of running water. A lover who always kept on his socks. Chariya—Mark would never say it—who cried after she made love, tears beading the small corners of her eyes. But not sad, she said, wiping her face and laughing. Not sad.

"I slept with a white man who kept asking me to talk to him in Hindi," Maya said.

"Did you?"

"Well, I don't know Hindi. So I just started saying the names of dishes in Indian restaurants."

"That's bad!" says Reggie. "What did he do?"

"He came."

The baby tires; Maya takes her and changes her and puts her to sleep. She stands tipsy in the dark room looking at the child with night-sharpened eyes. The child is curled, her fists, her feet, pulled tightly into herself, impenetrable in sleep. She looks fierce in her crib, giving the profound illusion of self-sustenance. Asking nothing from the young woman who looks down at her, and yet the question is posed anyway. Will she fly home with sleep knotted in her throat, go to work, and have drinks in bars, never marry, mourn alone? Will she remain in the company of these mourners, as the child grows more and more substantial and lovely, and learns the breadth and depth of her loss?

She cannot face this question. She wants to wake in her apartment and shake this dream off herself like a wet dog, take a shower, drink strong coffee, and sit in the bright possibility of morning. But morning will never come to her like that any longer. Each morning she will wake with the metallic tang of absence on her tongue.

In the kitchen Reggie helps Mark put away the dishes. But she is suddenly exhausted, and all at once the light in the room becomes white at the center and expands. The hand grasping the plate loosens and the plate shatters against the blue tile. She leans against the counter, until Mark's arms come around her and she slumps into the bulk of him, half-awake, half-dreaming, apologizing through furred lips. She can smell his swallowed tears but does not have the strength to feel pity. There is a bright buzzing in her body, the sound of a train. He lifts her above the shards of the plate, stepping carefully around them with his feet in only socks, calm, murmuring to her as he would to a child, saying she's very tired, she needs to rest. She has not been carried since she was a girl; Mark does it easily. For all her solidity and tallness, she is light in his arms as he puts her to bed. He inspects each calloused foot for embedded slivers of china, and when he finds none, asks her if she wants some water. "No," she says, waving him away. She says sorry. "Sorry for what?" She doesn't answer. Sleep hovers above her eyes with milky thickness. Then she has passed through, without a dream to soften it.

"Did she drink too much?" Maya says, standing in the doorway.

"She hardly had anything. She's just tired, I think."

"Should we call a doctor?"

"She's all right. Let her sleep."

They return to the kitchen and pick up the broken plate, Maya collecting the fat shards in a bag, Mark vacuuming the kitchen's little corners. When the task is finished, they leave the dishes where they are and open another bottle of wine. This bottle is better than the first; the bitterness feels expansive in their mouths. Maya's teeth get a bluish tint; Mark can see it when she smiles. There's a sugary scent coming off her skin, honey. "I remember the first time I met you. I didn't like you."

He is too tired to take it gamely. "Why not?"

"You seemed too golden. A little arrogant."

"I'd never been hurt before."

"But it's not better this way. You're not better. I wish you hadn't been hurt."

He says simply, "No point in wishing."

"You were kind to her."

She puts her foot on top of his foot under the table, and it's cold, he can feel it through his sock. Then she drops her eyes. Her hand rubbing absently the stem of her empty glass. It is a different man she met, six years ago, dressed smartly in a suit. As he has made no effort to dress these last few days; he has made no effort to guard and compose his face. Unshaven, the rough skin of a man, with freckles and creases. She can see the pores in his cheeks. She looks into his face like a palm reader looks at a hand, with a professional curiosity. And sees the future of the face, shock deepening into bitter anger. She sees love for the child spread thickly across the brow. The possibility of cruelty trembling in the tight corners of the mouth. She leans over the table and kisses the mouth softly. *Please do not be cruel.* The mouth is raw, as though she were kissing a wound. For a second their faces hover apart, their bodies are still, as if considering. Then she goes to him, crossing the distance of the table, bending her standing body to his, seated. The arms that take hold of her radiate from a desperate body. They go to Maya's room, not Mark's, and shut the door. She takes off the sweater that was Chariya's and the skirt and lies down on the bedspread. Mark standing over her, looking tender and hostile: a stranger. Her body feels crazy. *Please do not be cruel.* Looking at her, and she lets him look—at her body—but covers her face with the pillow. He pulls her to him and tugs her underwear down, looses the breasts from the bra, dark nipples bunching as they meet the blue air. Then he thrusts the smooth, warm length of himself into her, slicked with her wet, and she is gripping her legs around him. He lifts her up to him, their bodies pressed together, no space, finally, between their bodies, save for the tiny, infinite absence that stays between them, the questions the body asks and finds no answer to. Why? and Where? and Chariya?

Maya's eyes are open. She sees his ear, the curve of his head, the closed door. She can feel his anger coming through her like venom. But she will take it, his anger, and add it to her own. And warmth building at the center of her. She closes her eyes. Finds the body's comfort in another's, the sweat that gathers where they touch. She puts a hand against the back of his head, buries her fingers in the springy hair. Can he feel it, this warmth at the center, gentling? He becomes calm, even as his body reaches the frenzy. The feeling is almost holy. Her hair, loose, the honey smell coming all around him, falling over his shoulders. Her voice biting at his neck, building, building, then quieting. Joy from the body stumbles outward. They are stunned, scared by this joy. Yet each grasps it, holding it like a wild cat in the arms until it frees itself and bolts.

He puts her down on the bed. She, panting, looks at him. He is more humble than she has ever seen him. He has the urge to weep or to laugh.

"You want a cigarette?" he asks.

"I didn't know you smoked."

"Chariya made me quit. We'll have to go outside."

Maya pauses at the baby's door to check her sleeping. Her mouth is open, sucking. Mark and Maya put on scarves and hats and coats and step through the sliding door to the back porch. He draws a pack of cigarettes from his coat pocket and lights one cleanly. She sticks another, unlit, into her mouth and pretends to smoke. Still drunk.

"Can you feel her here?"

"Can you?"

She shakes her head. The cold burns at their fingertips. They're quiet for a while.

"There it is," he says, and points to the nest. Still bunched in the folds of the house like a tumor. "Will you come back?"

"Don't ask me that yet."

"Oh, have it," he says, rubbing the lighter into flame and holding it out to her. She cups her hand around it. Draws the nicotine deep into her, the tar. There is no moon out, but stars. She smoked cigarettes with Chariya. Home from college for Thanksgiving, and Chariya already working. Snuck booze and cigarettes into their parents' pristine house and giggled like wicked children. An animal noise pierces the dark:

the baby. It is Mark who tamps down the end of his cigarette and goes inside. Without switching on the light, he lifts her. It is a strange heft in his arms, his arms which have missed this weight. Chariya used to scold him, saying the baby would never learn to walk if he carried her everywhere.

"What is it?"

The baby quiets, becomes watchful. She can smell his cigarettes, but forgives him.

"She has a new tooth," says Maya, unwinding the scarf from her throat.

"How about that," he says to the child, rocking her, as the alcohol leaves his body. Soon she is asleep. The house is soaked in night: night has contracted like a fist around the house. No matter. They can light every lamp in the house until morning burns.

GHOST LOVER

BY LISA TADDEO

1. THE ONE AND ONLY

YOU'RE IN LINE AT the hipster sandwich place on a funereal block in the Hills, and you don't want to build your own. You could choose from one of the featured selections, but all are fattening. Pastrami is the polar opposite of Los Angeles.

You had wanted to make something yourself, avocado toast, for example, in your gleaming kitchen overlooking the Pacific. But you were out of avocados and there was only a quarter stick of butter left, which meant you couldn't yield anything toothsome. You could have had someone bring butter by, but that would have made you feel spoiled and flabby. And even though you would have wanted Kerrygold, you would probably have said, *Organic Valley or whatever, just no Land O'Lakes*. And the gofer would have texted no less than twice. *All they have is Breakstone's or Horizon?*

And you would have sat looking at the waves thawing on your

rocky bandage of beach in abject misery, waiting no less than three minutes so that the light-brown-haired girl who was younger and smaller and poorer than you would have had to tarry there, in the refrigerated section, wearing a sleeveless shirt on a gorgeous beach day, for you to reply, *Salted*. Sometimes the most you could do to make yourself happy was control another being. In the end, of course, it would never work out for you. You would always, for one, be fatter than you wanted to be. Controlling other people adds about five hundred calories. A delicious tropical drink at the bar next to Nobu on the PCH has one hundred more calories if you're trying to make your assistant pay for the fact that you are on a bad date, by texting her while she is on a good one.

In line at the sandwich shop, you open a bag of Caesar Twice-Baked Croutons. If you eat only half the bag, it will be 170 calories. There is a fly, large and slowed by the greatness of late summer, coasting low. A couple in front of you is playful. Leaning in, the young man inhales the midsection of the girl's hair. She turns to meet his eyes, smiling. They don't hear the fly, which is buzzing loud at ear height. When the lovemaking gaze breaks, the boy turns and notices you. At first he barely registers you, because you are not hot and his girlfriend is. And then he recognizes you. He punches his girl in the arm.

Hey! he says. *Hey*! It's—You're Ari the Ghost Lover! Right?

You feel dizzy, the crouton in your mouth the size of a nightmare. You try to chew it quietly but there is no quiet, fast way to get rid of a crouton. There is only slow disintegration.

The girlfriend widens her eyes in apparent recognition. The fly whirs past. Behind you, the sooty screen door opens and shuts and you take the opportunity to turn your head in its direction, and chomp the crouton.

Oh my god, says the girl. It's you!

You turn back to them. Flecks of dried parsley on your lips. She wears a sleeveless *Cure* shirt without a bra, and her side-boob slaloms around Robert Smith's ear. Her shoulders are smooth and round. She is twenty-five. You were never twenty-five.

You're the reason my best friend is getting married to, like, the guy of her dreams! says the girl.

The boy smirks. *Luke* is the guy of her dreams?

The girl punches him and rolls her eyes. They both turn to you.

No shit! We're going to their wedding in, like, two months! It's all because of you!

You smile, though you don't mean to. You imagine the girl's best friend is probably a Tier III customer. Although this could have come just from watching your show. It is the only self-help show that has ever been binge-watched, on Netflix. This is something Jennifer, your PR girl, says more often than she says her own name.

Oh my god, Pandora is going to shit herself when we tell her we met you!

The boy, by now, has lost interest. He is scraping the meat of the girl's waist with his fingernails. Her black jeans are low-waisted. Her hip bone is a seat belt. All he wants to do is fuck her. You are more adept at reading this, you know, than anybody in the whole world.

You are amazing. You are, like, my hero.

You nod. You resolved a week ago to stop saying thank you. To be icier in general. The decision was made on a day that your sliding door was open to your balcony and a strange bird whined in the distance.

The noise of him made you want to pluck his eyes out, and your own. On that day you were the furthest from God you had ever been. You'd never believed in him, but on that day you could feel the whole ocean freeze. You felt your toes go bloodless. That was the day the card arrived, sailing forth over the tender shoots.

Can I—can we, like, get your autograph, I don't know, or something?

The boy doesn't care, not at all. The fact that the girl cares more about meeting you than she cares about her boyfriend in this moment makes you hate her very much, for having that power. She is lucky. A blind providence afforded her at birth, by how big her eyes are and how tall her cheekbones. At home the screen door is off its track. There is no one you can ask to fix this. There is someone, but you can't ask him to fix it yet. You know it is too soon. That it always will be.

Next, can I help you! the sandwich guy yells.

It's Sunday, which for you is a whale's throat. Blue-black and forever. People always write and call you on Monday mornings, at 10:27, when you are the busiest. On Sunday, almost never. Not even the old high-school friends whose husbands have a rare form of cancer, and who are looking for a handout. Even those people are too full in their lives to ping you on a Sunday.

The girl and the boy turn to the sandwich guy. Uh, one roast pork banh mi and one TOAO grilled cheese, says the boy.

You remember the first time you came here, and it was with him. He showed you LA like he was opening a sunlit door through his chest. His sandwich place. Scummy but redolent with the smell of half-cooked bread, on a hill over the highway, canopied by trees. The bottles of wine inside, for sale. You could go home with a bottle of wine, and sandwiches.

No tomatoes on the grilled cheese, the girl whispers, tugging at the boy's soft gray shirt.

No tomatoes on The One And Only, he says to the sandwich guy, who nods.

Twenty even, the sandwich guy says. The boy pulls a twenty out of his pocket. It looks like the last twenty on earth, and your heart breaks a little more, when into the boy's shoulder blade the girl whispers, Thank you.

2. THE FUTURE IS FEMALE

On the way to the Country Mart, you dial the temperature down to sixty, and draw the flow to the max. Within seconds your face is chilled like a tumbler of milk. You used to worry about how much gasoline the air conditioning was using. Now you don't anymore. When your cheeks are cold, they feel thinner.

It has been almost two years now. In two years you have become something utterly different from what you were, at least to the wider world. It didn't know you at all before, and now almost everyone does. This is a crazy feeling. Men in Titleist hats and flaccid golf shirts know who you are, because their daughters do. Because your face is all over the place. You are rich. That word! You bought a house in Malibu. On stilts, with one of those driveways, right off the PCH. You used to say, This is not so great. *This* is Malibu? And Nick would say, You have no idea, the other side. And one day he took you to walk along the other side, over the rocks along the breathing water, and you could see the decks and the real fronts of the houses. The fronts were facing the ocean! The *other* side, the *highway* side: that was the back.

When you were on the ocean side, you understood how much more these people knew than you did, had than you did. He held your hand over the sharp rocks. You don't remember wanting more then, but you must have.

Your house is an A-frame. You lied to your best friend about how much it cost, because you felt bad paying for the place in cash when she was struggling, with two jobs, to pay off her nursing school loans. There is a terrific white bathroom on the topmost floor. A claw-foot bathtub, with golden spigots, overlooking the water. Heaven-white towels on teak rods and a bar of soap on the teak stool. Vetiver with French green clay, still wrapped in its furred paper.

You are on your way to the Country Mart right now, for an iced matcha latte and to buy clothes at the sorts of prices that still beguile you. You can spend over two thousand dollars on a sheer blouse that still requires something to go underneath it. The less one's body is perfect, the more it needs expensive garments, heavy crepes to position themselves like aid workers across the fault lines.

Still, the old ways cling. The soap in your bathroom is an eighteen-dollar bar. You refuse to use it until you have lost at least five pounds.

The idea for Ghost Lover came, sorely, from Nick. Or, rather, from the dissolution of Nick and you. There was an insolvency. The opposite of an impalement. You defecated your soul, is how you marked it at the time, in less refined language, across the pages of your journal. You mourned for months and then you sat in coffee shops and strategized. At first you planned to get him back. There was one coffee shop in particular, on La Cienega, a place untouched by him, someplace he never would have noted. It wasn't precious enough, or clean. There were no whole

Arabica beans for sale. There was a fifty-something lady who worked in the kitchen there, and she also came around and tidied up the packets of sugar substitute and hand-swept the milk counter. At first you hated the grunts she made. You hated how shapeless her butt was and how noisy her shoes were. You hated the way she stalked behind you, her toes at your heels like dominos. You were sure that, even though she did not seem to speak English, she was reading the words on your laptop. Your journal entries. Then one day, as she mopped around your chair, she placed her hand on your shoulder. Hallowed, like a mother or a priest. It wholed you. You turned, and her ancient eyes absorbed your depth.

Just like that, everything settled. And you thought, I am fine. I will send him a note. It was his birthday. You wrote, *Happy Birthday.* Sending the words across the avenues of code, you felt like a queen of love. Seven minutes later he replied, *Thx!*

A week later, Nick walked into your coffee shop. With a girl. A definitive girl, about a decade younger. You passed gas when you saw him. The girl turned in the direction of the sound, and found you. Her face bloomed rose with compassion. He didn't seem to have heard. And she didn't know who you were; she didn't know how once Nick ate you out in your mother's house while Karl, the husband of hers who used to violate you, listened from downstairs.

Importantly, Nick hadn't noticed you, so you ran out, without your computer or your pile of books. You sweated around a corner until they left, in *her* car, which was sporty and black. This made you feel sick. Something about him being in a girl's car. Listening to her young music. When you went back in, the woman was standing by your table, protecting your stuff with her shadow. She nodded at you. You wanted to cry. You knew you would not come back, would never see her again. These tiny endings are all over the place.

Ghost Lover came easily from there, ideas borne from pain the way moths go to light. You quit your job as the second assistant to a midlevel celebrity. A job you had gotten only to have a reason to be in LA, with him. You began sleeping during the days, through iced drinks in fraternal sunlight and blondes in bathing suits playing volleyball. You'd go out only at night. Sit in Chez Jay, which had been his but which you had stolen. You felt the greasy luxe of being somewhere you shouldn't. The creepiness of lying in wait. You listened. Girls with text messages, mainly. How to respond to this one or that one. They didn't know anything. They were young and pointless. But you felt for them, or, rather, you felt for the pain in them. Or no. Your pain felt a kinship to their pain, and at the time you had to be wherever your pain was. It was the only thing that was real.

One night there you ran into an old friend of yours from home, who was pursuing an accelerated MBA in Long Beach and cheating on his girlfriend nearly every weekend. You continued on to drinks and food at Father's Office. The sweetness of the burger was pink and wrong on your tongue. You sensed he just wanted a place to sleep over in LA. But he was useful, like many ancillary characters; you didn't realize how much, until later. He said the only thing you actually learn in business school is "identify a problem in the marketplace and create a solution."

That night you ingested over 2,500 calories, at the bar and later at home. You took an Ambien and wrote a business plan until the words melted across the screen. You slept with the friend in business school the next weekend. He felt like a soft iron inside of you, something plain and graceless. The dumb pain of simple rod sex. You did not come. He ejaculated largely inside your belly button. The fatty pool of it.

Several weeks later, with this friend's help, you created the application. A forwarding system for text messages so that an expert would respond (or not respond) to a client's crush. The client would be briefed as needed, would otherwise enjoy holy ignorance. A way for girls, mainly, to be the coolest versions of themselves, inoculated in practice against their desire.

At first the expert was only you. You, thinking of how Nick himself would respond to a text. How the young and beautiful girls he was newly with would respond to the texts of grunting men. Quickly, your team grew. You hired small, stunning girls. You always brought on women you imagined him wanting. One of the reasons was for the angry throb it drew from your pelvis. Another was so that you would never invite him back into your life. You could not, feasibly, because there were too many limbs for you to be jealous of. All that superlative hair, all those surfing thighs.

3. BEAUTIFUL WITHOUT LOOKING LIKE YOU'RE TRYING

There are the girls who please girls, and the girls who please boys. Girls who please girls, even at thirteen—what they do is they blow a boy not to make the boy like them but to go back and report to their girls. The taste and flavor, checking a box. You were in the second group. You always fell hard for boys. Each one was his own fairy tale. One therapist said you got this from observing your mother. Another said it was a by-product of your father's death.

Right now there is one, Jeff. He is a photographer. You have been bringing him to parties. Events that require bow ties. He is always perfumed and ready on time. You know who was never ready on time.

You're at the Country Mart to buy a dress for one such event, at the Getty Villa tonight. You come here because you cannot stomach downtown LA. Rodeo, with its chalky sunlight. And the malls are out of the question. You have grown past the malls. Your tastes have become ultra-refined. You are hopeful today about Morgane Le Fay. You are imagining something breezy and decently transparent.

With this new one you are more worried than usual. Jeff has acquired some gentle fame via you. You suggested him as the photographer for your *Elle* shoot. He didn't want to do the lighting their way, and then he did. Since then, he has booked gigs for *Vogue* and *Esquire*. You heard him on the phone with a girl from *W*, negotiating and charming. Jennifer, your publicist, called him "hot" to both your faces. This was vaguely unforgivable, but you forgave it. Privately, to you, and early on enough that she could pretend it never happened, she questioned his motives. You met him on a site for people with more than ten thousand Twitter followers. Either you were hot or you had a certain number of Twitter followers. You were in the latter group. He was in the first.

In the store a salesgirl recognizes you. Even in your sunglasses and Bruins hat. You have a pug nose. It is unmistakable. To be recurrently recognized for an element of unattractiveness is a scorching feeling. It makes you want to punish every brown-haired beauty in your path.

Jennifer is the other reason you are doggedly spotted. She is better at her job than anyone you have ever met. It's mostly accidental. Like all huge successes, she had a few dead-on things happen and now she merely capitalizes on her reputation.

Are you... Wow. It's you.

You don't even nod at her. Sometimes when you eat too much at lunch you need to be cruel to a salesgirl. You finger a flowing cream dress. She offers to start a fitting room for the zero items you have in your hand.

She says a few more things, platitudes both empty and necessary, but when she asks if you are looking for anything special, you snap.

No, in fact. I'm looking for something really un-special. Tell me. What is the *least* special thing you have in the store?

Back outside, you close your eyes against the sun and smush your temples. Oh, the indignity of Sunday!

You open your eyes and send Jennifer a quick text.

I was a mild bitch at Morgane Le Fay.

Montana or Malibu? Customer or salesgirl?

Latters, you write. This is how good you are at your job. You are a clinician of the text. You can eviscerate, palpate, abrogate with a mild word, combined with cunning punctuation. You want Jennifer to have to ask someone what you mean. You want her to feel dumb, undeserving. Like the PR girl that she is. Lest she mistake her thinness for value.

Having bought nothing, you walk back to the car. The sandy mountains in the distance used to confound you. On the one hand, they looked like nature and wild, but then all these boat-shaped villas had wedged themselves into the more hospitable rocks. The houses appeared white and dirty from below, but they were all gated. Nobody used the land they owned. There were horses, but they were dry and hot. The hills of Los Angeles used to confound you, but now you've been to parties in those neglected palaces. You have seen swimming pools used as swan ponds and naked-man ponds. You have seen swimming pools that have never been filled with water. When you are inside the mountains, you realize they are not mountains but placeholders.

You wake up your car and use the key to turn on the AC before you get in. You will wear the red dress that Nick bought you at that consignment shop in Cambridge. All these years later, all these diets later, you are still mostly the same size. If only people knew how much work went into your weight. The fluctuations in your mind rocket and plunge like an ambitious water slide. Your relationship with your refrigerator has given the cat an anxiety disorder. But on your body the movements are razor bumps.

Anyway, the dress still fits; it's the only one in which you have ever felt effortlessly beautiful.

You will be accepting an award tonight, to become the third annual Golda Meir Ambassador for Women. You have a speech to deliver to a room of very important people. At first you were going to talk about coming from mostly nothing into a lot of something. Nothing anybody hadn't heard before. You were embarrassed by the banality, but you are so starlit right now that it doesn't matter, not even to you.

Then the card arrived. And your bowels released themselves, melt- ingly, like a spoon of honey submerged in tea.

You took a long eucalyptic bath. You changed your speech completely.

4. THE OLD PLACE WITH THE NEW GUY

You are meeting Jeff for drinks, before the awards. For his thirty-third birthday, last month, you bought him a heritage-green Triumph and he loves riding it through the canyons. Lately he has suggested meeting you out, instead of driving with you. You told him you didn't mind the motorcycle, that you weren't scared. But he said he was, about being a novice and getting you hurt. Anyway, tonight it's a moot point, because of your hair and the wind, and your dress.

The Old Place is another place Nick took you. It was the week you first visited, when you staked your claim. You expressed sadness about the oceans of macadam and the squat buildings. You'd imagined all of Los Angeles was like one or two streets in Beverly Hills, palm-lined and arugula-grassed. Nick said, Los Angeles is not what anybody thinks it is, before they get here. That's because it doesn't actually exist. You have to make your own LA.

Then he took you to the Old Place in his Subaru. It was terrific. A remote, weedy heaven, a warty barn with antlers on the front and horseshoes inside and oil lamps and carved-up wooden tables. It looked like Wyoming and yet there was a Spanish-style villa just around the bend, and a constellation of Teslas. Inside, you shared a charcuterie board and counted your quarters. Your waitress, who was beautiful, didn't scare you. You and he were still only friends then. It was a year after college. The Boston years, he used to say; one year on from Boston.

But even then, it was bigger for you. In your journals, there is a red star sticker on the night you met. It was the spring of your junior year and the cops had just busted a party at the Towers. You held a Solo cup in your hand that you didn't know what to do with.

Nick had met you earlier at the keg. He'd pumped and poured one for you, asking if you liked head. Your eyes widened. On your beer, he said.

As the cops squared their hips at you, he assessed your predicament, ripped off his shirt, and bared his chest to them, like Tarzan. It's easy for beautiful people to disrobe and cause this sort of diversion. In any case, you fell for an act of humanity in someone hot.

Jeff, who has become Jeffrey lately in his magazine work, texts that he is leaving now, ten minutes before you are supposed to meet. It will take him forty minutes to come from his studio downtown. He has a drawer at your place, and will sleep over. In the morning he'll go for a run on the beach, and return shirtless. He always leaves a neutral James Perse hanging from the point of a certain rock. He is like an actor in some ways. You'll have showered and applied an invisible amount of makeup and made fresh cashew milk. He'll come in and press his waist to yours and kiss you on the cheek, and you'll want him again. But he always has to go. He is always working, unless there is an event.

It's four when you get there. You choose the same table from nearly a decade ago. A waitress comes by, in her fifties and pockmarked. You order a vodka soda and scan the menu for something with less than a hundred calories. There are no oysters. No ceviche. The better the atmosphere of a bar, especially one in the woods, the more fried the food will be.

You check Jeff's Instagram, because sometimes he will take a picture of somewhere you don't even know he is. His account is a mix of scenic, foggy photographs—glassy bodies of water and tall trees in sunlight—and selfies of you and him, at awards shows and on private jets and in Cannes and in the Côte d'Azur. There is one picture that makes you die. You and him at Alexander McQueen, during New York Fashion Week. You are in a purple dress that Jennifer said made you look like a goddess. He is tan and his face is weak but still undeniably handsome. Someone neither of you knew commented, *Still Life of Photographer, and a Sausage in Balmain.*

You asked him to make his account private that night. Of course, he said. You asked him again in the morning.

Nine years ago, at this very table, you told Nick about Karl. Karl wore glasses and had slick, curly hair and oh, how your mother loved him.

You told Nick all of it. How you made the fucker pay, literally, for every transgression. For the time that he fingered you in the hallway when you were coming out of the shower in your Kensie Girl robe, you used his credit card to buy a pair of Prada sunglasses. When he placed your hand over his dick under the table while your mom sat directly across from you? You bought your gay friend Bobby a dinner jacket.

You didn't tell Nick about Karl to get it off your chest. You told him about Karl so that he might love you.

Jeff comes in, helmet in hand. He smiles at the bartender and quizzes the empty room. He sees you, and then he finds you.

Babe, he says, kissing you across the table.

Hey, you say flatly. You have perfected austerity at surprising moments. It keeps people feeling like they have wronged you, and thinking they need to overcompensate.

You look unbelievable.

Thanks.

Are you all set? Any nerves I can tend to? Do they have a teleprompter, or are you going off the cuff?

Off the cuff.

You are a *beast*.

I need to tell you about what I'm going to say.

Give it to me, he says, waggling his finger for the waitress. He is obsequiously polite with waitstaff, yet also urgent.

It's about my ex.

Whoa, he says.

It's about how my ex raped me.

Jeff is the starched breed of new man. He has ridden horses in Texas like a cowboy but the word *rape* gives him menstrual cramps. He doesn't know the most politically correct way to handle this. Mostly, he does not act from his heart.

He gasps. The waitress comes around and he is too ruffled to order his drink. He shakes his head. You order it for him.

He'll have a vodka grapefruit, you say.

Absolut okay? she says.

Grey Goose, he whispers. To you, he says, *What do you mean?*

You inhale deeply. It's a complex thing, you say, like all these things are. We were together for a long time. We were very much in love. He was definitely forceful. Arguments we got into. But otherwise, no red flags. He was—I thought he was a good guy.

Jeff nods and shakes his head. Riveted.

You tell him about the night you intend to discuss in your speech. You and Nick were both on mushrooms, but he was unused to psychedelics. He was a beer guy. Your friend Bobby had mailed them to you, for your birthday. With Karl's Amex you paid for a bungalow at the Beverly Hills Hotel. You and Nick went out and had drinks at Slumulous with a bunch of his friends because you didn't have your own yet. He didn't want to take the mushrooms, but it was your birthday and you insisted.

Nine years ago, at this table, when you told Nick about Karl, he said he was going to kill him. Please, you said, crying. Please, it's over. I just need—

What? Nick was pissed.

You wanted to say, *I just need* you. Instead you let the pain cramp your features.

Jeff reaches his smooth hand across the table to hold yours. You are steady and alpha and also afraid that you look ugly.

At some point, in the middle of the night, he climbed on top of me. He was a big guy. Not fat, just. Very broad, and toned and muscular. He got on top of me and sort of ripped my underwear to the side, like stretched them out. Sorry. Then he started, like, pumping away. Like he was trying to core me.

Oh my god.

I mean, it woke me up. And I knew. I knew he was fucked-up. Like, he didn't even know what he was doing. I don't think. It was over before I could even stop it. I don't know how to describe that.

No, I get it.

Of course you do.

Back when, Nick had said, Tell me what the fucker looks like. This was before old people had Facebook. No, you said. I don't know. He's. He looks like someone you wouldn't think was capable. Of doing that.

When Jeff comes inside of a condom inside of you, you can feel his medium-sized penis begin to contract long before his orgasm has crested. Something tells you this wouldn't happen to him with a hooker. The waitress brings his drink and places it far enough from his hand that he needs to reach, in the middle of you speaking.

I think it's important, you say, to tell these women tonight. They deserve to know. I think it will help them come forward with their own experiences. Every woman has an experience like this. *At least* one.

Jeff nods expansively.

I wanted to prepare you. I know that it might be uncomfortable.

No, Ari. I am here for you. I am here for whatever you need and. I just can't believe this happened to you. That you have been living with this. Secret.

The way Nick responded about Karl was wild and bucking. It made you feel like a flamenco dancer, like a woman worthy of killing for.

You sip your drink until it is gone. Jeff orders another because it is all just too much, this information, this evening. The waitress seems to know to bring you the bill. That always happens lately.

5. BECAUSE THE NIGHT

The outdoor theater at the Getty is half-Shakespearean, half–dingy Malibu. Accordingly, you feel tan and legitimate. The vodka soda on an empty stomach was one hair thicker than the perfect amount of inebriation, which is actually even more perfect. You have always been able to alchemize a wrong into a positive. It's one of the ways you got here.

Even the card last week. *Especially* the card. You are about to turn it on its head.

The bar is still being set up and only the important people are here. You, the First Lady, the other speakers, the editors of the major women's magazines, the president of the International Council of Women. Jeff is very good at being unobtrusive. He is not one of those boyfriends who stand in your limelight. He always positions himself just off to the side, so that the glow strikes him well. Cameras always wonder who he is that way; they crane, and he smiles.

Ari, you look gorgeous! says the editor in chief of *W*. Her dress is spangled and violent. Elvira shoulders, St. Pauli Girl décolletage. Rhinestones in the shape of matadors.

You hate when people say, *You* look *beautiful*. That is cruel. *Tonight, with that dress and the professional hair and makeup, you nearly pass for one of us. We are proud of you. Welcome, and here is some mesclun.*

You are the second-most important person here tonight. You radiate the consummate mix of celebrity and public service required to achieve American glory. You are at the height of your likability. It is minute by minute, of course, but nobody wants to tear you down yet. The denouement will come, yes, but then you can abscond to Greece, Lithuania. You can kill yourself.

But for now, you have arrived. Look at that theater! Soon it will be stocked with broken women in four-hundred-dollar dresses and ten-thousand-dollar jumpsuits. The socioeconomic gamut of coastal American style. You see a woman compensating for acne with a short beige dress. She has nice legs but will never shake the agony of her skin. She is your sister but you have risen above her. You had lain in wait, a snake in the grass, planning for this. To be huge. You didn't think it would be about him. You were over it, you said to no one. But you are not. If there had been any doubt that you were still in the undertow, all doubt was expelled Monday morning.

It was classy, of course, because he was elegantly simple and probably the girl is too. Brown like a bear. Heavy stock. Raised white letters. "Save the Night."

Not a whole thing, no churches and bearers and limousines. Just a band, drinks, the people they love.

The people we love.

As though you were friends. Yes, you have kept in touch like friends throughout the years. He'd gone back to Boston and you liked him there. He was safe from blondes in bikinis. From salesgirls in white jeans and baristas in T-strap tank tops. He congratulated you on every milestone, the first time you appeared on Friedkin, and on the cover of *Wired*. Of course he was even more excited to see you on the cover of *Boston Magazine*. He texted you a picture of it, magnetized to his fridge. You felt warm in your belly that day, eating only kale and apples.

You saw him as recently as eighteen months ago, when you went home for Karl's funeral. Karl got hit by a car, outside the bar he went to every Thursday with the boys. You were thrilled, but not for the reasons one might think.

For the wake your mother wore her hair in a strangling bun, and the blackest dress you had ever seen. You never told her about Karl. She either knew or she didn't. Anyway, you knew what would happen if the information came from you. You remembered with baleful clarity the trip you took to Destin, just you and her, months after your father died and right before Karl. You were twelve; you hated your hair and had a sickening crush on Douglas Greenway. At the pool of your dated motel, your mother lay on a chaise longue, in an emerald bathing suit and big sunglasses, keeping her body straight and tight in a way you had never seen. You sat at the corner of her chair, blue, but not blocking her sun.

What is it? she said.

You missed your father but sensed you shouldn't say this. You also missed the boy. He didn't love you, yet. But you felt you deserved something. You knew people so deeply.

I was just. Missing Douglas.

Does he even like you? said your mother. You understood she was not looking at you, even though she was wearing sunglasses.

I don't know, you told her honestly. He went to the movies with Amber and her mom last week.

You were deaf from the pool water. You'd spent the morning doing leg lifts in the shallow end. Then handstands and hoping your legs looked nice, at twelve. It was 3:00 p.m. and you were thinking how long it would be until bedtime, and dreading the darkness at the same time. Florida was all pink clamshells and depression, malls with skylights and surplus palms. Old people, jobless and white. Plus, you were in the worst part of it. This motel, this town, not-Miami. A polyp on a turd. The blue of the pool was a cheap blue. It had a urine cast. The sun here was cheap too.

Your mother inhaled through her nose. She'd been drinking Bloody Marys since noon. This last one had stretched itself into peppery red water. The ice was melted. The celery looked warm.

I hope you never have a boy, she said, finally. You'll be jealous of his babysitters.

Nick called the day you landed. He wouldn't come to the funeral, but he asked you to Fisherman's Feast. This was right before you'd shot up to intergalactic level, before you'd reached ten thousand followers. You had a nice tan, wore a Cubs hat, and remembered when merely walking through aisles of fried dough with frizzy hair and a boyfriend was enough. He looked dreamy and broad, and cozy like pizzerias in

October. And you thought, This could be forever. We could have a child, and Septembers.

Tripe, yelled a busker. Just got here!

Nick said, Can we get two pounds, rare?

You wrinkled your nose and he ran away. The busker stared at you, presenting a length of tender blond loofah.

You caught up to him and punched his arm. It was hard and present. You remembered the first time you had cracked him. When it went from him making you laugh to him making sure he had made you laugh. Had Karl helped? Yes. Karl had helped.

Later, walking down Beacon in some bourbon-colored sunshine, you said, Why does Edible Arrangements have a storefront still?

You had been planning all day to ask him if he wanted to get dinner. You felt nervous but optimistic. You had eaten perfectly. One banana. Three snakeskin slices of turkey. But otherwise you hadn't prepared at all.

I think that kind of hope is beautiful, he said.

He stopped walking and looked at you. He asked if you were okay. He meant about Karl. His obsession with how the Karl situation affected you was a Bruce Springsteen song.

Hey! you said. How about me and you in LA? Do you ever think about those days?

Oh, man, do I. We were fucking toxic.

But also fucking great, I think.

He laughed, shining his big neck back at the sun, and said, It's crazy. I can't even imagine us, you know, being intimate. I think we were always meant to be the best of friends.

He ruffled your hat. The sky turned black. You utterly lost your shit. Your face overheated. You felt round and faint. There was no way to go back in time, no way to make him unsay that thing that you could never unhear. Your guts were rivering into your bowels. You ran away from him before you shit yourself. You ran all the way home.

You ate that night with your mother, frozen shepherd's pies, funeral cupcakes brought by women who'd never lost a soul. Karl's empty mid-century chair at the table, everything unheated and ended.

You returned to LA in the morning, three days early. Like always, you regrouped. You ramped up the plan. Purpose bubbled like black fish in your blood.

"Become More Beautiful" you wrote at the top of the vision board.

But you couldn't do that. So you became everything else.

Karl had left you two hundred and fifty thousand dollars. Honestly, it felt worth it. It was a good price. You grew your company by 1.5. You hired Jennifer. The Netflix show came unexpectedly. A wise-voiced man rang you up and offered it, and overnight you became this sensation.

Everything was going swimmingly. There was a plan in place, both heuristic and magical. You were going to lose fifteen pounds and see Nick again over Christmas. There was a certain amount of success that would make him unable to refuse you. There was a certain weight at which he would think you were pretty.

But then last week you got the card.

You went to meet her on Facebook. She is Nick's friend Gordon's younger sister. Young and small and honey haired. You had heard that description of hair before, and it seemed trite. But this girl has honey hair.

She graduated from Harvard—where you did not get in—just two years ago. You clicked through the available pictures. One of her in a sports bra and eggplant yoga pants. She is a runner. She likes Adidas sneakers and the *Atlantic Monthly*. She likes Jean-Luc Godard and George Eliot and Prince.

Honey hair. Fawn hair. She used the phrase *Damascan rose* in the caption of a picture. She is not funny but she is not an idiot. One of her brothers is a pilot. Both of her parents are alive.

Because she has a private profile, and because Nick is not on Facebook, you had to be crafty to find pictures of the two of them. You moused through Gordon's girlfriend's account. There was the golden cache. A double-date weekend to a tiny house in the woods, one of those hipster getaways. She is in big, soft, black sweatpants and his sweatshirt. She is in jeans and a plaid shirt. She is roasting a marshmallow in a black knit dress and a tartan afghan. The moon is a bone in the shape of a hole. He is looking at her in every single picture.

You masturbated to these images, to the concatenation of his newfound happiness and your old happiness, now dashed. Then, needing more, you went on YouPorn, selected the category "Romantic," selected the sub-category "Beautiful fucking." There you found a gorgeous honey-haired French girl in a sun-filled farmhouse slicing apples in a plaid shirt. A man comes up behind her.

After you came, you contemplated suicide in the boring, lonely way of unfulfilled, selfish women. But that was last week. You have regrouped (again!). Look at the theater!

Karl used to sweat over you. He was working so hard, he was sweating. The nervousness, it must have been. He kept his shoes on, in case your mom came home and he had to motor. So you would just concentrate on the shoes, pattering against your own naked feet. Deer-colored bucks. Like a schoolboy. Very clean, never rained upon.

Now you are going to thank the beaten and sexually abused women of the world, really *all* the women of the world, for this award, for your general success, which would not have been possible without them, for your belief in the collective future of womankind, and you are going to tell them what Nick did. It won't be televised, but by the morning all the news outlets will have picked it up. You won't name him but you will provide enough details that his community will be able to figure it out. Certainly the girl will. You don't think about his mother. You don't think about the things he planted in the ground for you.

Things you won't talk about from that psychedelic night at the Beverly Hills Hotel:

You won't talk about the kissing;

the way your hips rose to meet his on hydraulics;

the way you grabbed his rear harder than you ever had, because you were safe in the pea soup of a drug;

that you *wished* you'd been asleep, that you wished you could sleep through anything to do with him;

that it was the best night of your life. The best sex, with anyone, even with him. Because in the dark you felt loved and wanted, more than you loved or wanted him; that you were both on drugs, yes, but that nothing he did was forceful. Nothing he ever did was forceful. The only thing that was different was the way he seemed to want you. Like it was the very first time he'd truly fucking wanted you, as much as or more than he cared about you or felt pity for you or felt friendship for you; how in the morning you jokingly said, You raped me last night!

How he said, That's not even funny.

Because you can get arrested?

No, he said. Ari. He said your name like someone who loved you but was not obsessed with you. Like someone who might take care of you forever, if you were open to denial.

Please. I want to pretend he doesn't exist.

One day he won't, he said.

You ate red and black berries on the sunny patio of the bungalow that morning and read the paper together, but the fear had crept in and was sitting on the wrought-iron bench beside you, your own ghost lover that only you could see. You were always anticipating the day Nick would leave, a pit in your stomach that didn't even keep you feeling full. You knew that he would. So you decided then to leave him first. Would any of these women tonight believe that of all the things in your life that had happened to you—the death of your father and the sixty-seven times you were palmed or swathed or entered against your will by a man with *tendrils* for hair—leaving Nick was actually the hardest thing you had ever done?

The president of the council introduces you, and you take the stage to TLC's "No Scrubs." In the third row, Jennifer stands in an emerald jumpsuit, her arms folded importantly, as everyone else claps. She has taken up beside an Argentinean model who is dating America's sexiest man alive. Like the rest of them, Jennifer is a star-fucker. She thinks people on a screen are more valuable than she is. Maybe you know better, but you are no better. You have learned that the only thing superior to family is people who make money off your success. It makes you reach for the stars. We all need somebody to please.

Jeff claps aggressively on the other side of Jennifer. He is very dapper and his beard looks painted on, from this distance. You feel unmoved at the idea of him, suddenly. Your desire is at absolute zero. Conversely, you always wanted Nick. Even in the effervescing moments right after an orgasm. You'd always had trouble coming with a man, but never with him. During Karl but before Nick, you envisioned your clitoris lying on cement, sped over flickeringly by bicycle wheels. It would regenerate itself and look alive again, but its soul was smashed, bleeding tiny ruby seahorse tears on the sidewalks outside your father's home.

Then Nick made you come through your heart. You didn't need anything else.

All these women will listen, because you have all of their ears. Because you have shown them how to win men, you may now show them how to win themselves. It's time to flip the switch. Paths of celebrity need to be redirected every six months to keep relevant.

It will be a good thing! Because women will come forward, about their own fingerings and their own *just the tip*s, *just for a minute*s, their own predators and assholes and buck-footed mothers' husbands.

Oh, but still you will let yourself hope. Even after the program this evening, when the nail is in the coffin, so to speak. Like you keep the wrapped soap in the bathroom, you are always saving for a sunny afternoon. Perhaps one day, if the world is emptied by zombies, if all the things that shouldn't matter no longer do, then you will tell him, *I'm sorry. I'm sorry.*

You will cry into his chest. You will forsake the fame, the money, the stilted house, the chilled, silver car.

To what devil did you promise your soul? It's no longer a promise. He has it now. He is spinning it into a pink fever, like cotton candy. It's too late. Look at the theater. Look down at your glass-heeled shoes, which cost nine hundred dollars. Touch your perfect hair that smells of nice hotels.

Imagine, if you want, the future. You have enough money that you can envision any development and deem it possible.

In the future, he will tuck your hair behind your ears, like he used to, his fingers large and full of grace, and say, *It's okay.*

He will understand; he will understand that these people would not pity you for what your stepfather did. Or they would for a night and then they would think you are gross. They would think about you what you have often thought about yourself. In the shower, when you are scrubbing your thighs. Your stepfather made you lust after soap, made you want to slough the tainted gum of your uterus.

But Nick was a man, a *man*, and real men forgive. Look at your boyfriend there, useless in Armani. It's possible, you see, that Nick was the only good man in America. But it was never going to happen unless you did these millions of terrible things. You are looking at this rayon rainbow and in your head you are saying this as a mantra. Like a series of locks clicking into place. Like stepping twice inside this square, and skipping these three cracks. Thank god nobody can see inside your head! You clear your throat of pain and useless trepidation and address the auditorium of showered women:

Ladies, you will say. *And gentlemen.*

Los Angeles will be still for you. So will Boston. Your mother, finally, will listen.

It's okay, Nick will whisper, at the other end of this moonless night. *I can take the hit. It will be our little secret.*

Because, he will say, looking at you for the first time like you are a dancer and not a fighter, *because this is how much I love you.*

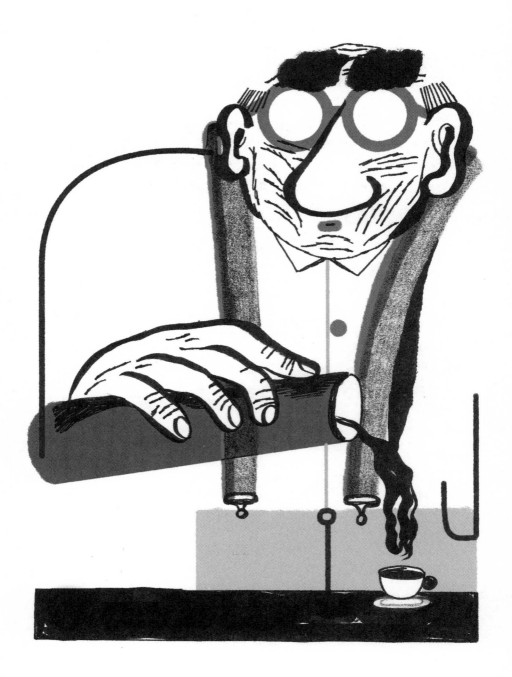

TODAY

BY STEPHEN DIXON

SO TODAY SHE DIED. Seven years ago today. In her hospital bed at home.
I was sitting beside her. Opened her eyes, made a growling sound, half
closed her eyes, raised her head a little, head sank back into the pillow,
and she died. The phone rang. I said, "Hello," thinking it was the hospice nurse saying what time she'd be coming over this morning. It was
my friend in Paris.

"Victor, it's Paul. How are things?"

I said, "Pamela just died."

"Oh, no," he said.

"Just a minute ago. Less."

"I'm so sorry I called. So sorry for you."

"It's all right," I said. "You didn't know. I have to cut this short and
wake up my daughter."

"Of course," he said. "I'll never feel good again as to what I've done today. I was calling to see how she is. I'm so sorry."

"Excuse me, but I have to hang up now."

I go into the room she died in. The hospital bed was removed the day after she died. The room went back to being the guest room. I bought a double bed a few weeks later, same bed that's there now. She's asleep in that bed. I don't want to wake her. This is going nowhere. I pull the paper out of the typewriter, tear it up, go to the kitchen, and dump the pieces into the recycling bag next to the trash can. I pour myself some coffee from the thermos. Made the coffee about an hour ago. I've had breakfast. I've read part of today's newspaper. I didn't sleep well last night or early this morning. Total sleep of about three hours. My stomach hurts. I feel constipated but I had a normal bowel movement yesterday. It all has to do with today, I'm sure. It'll be a tough day to get through. I'll speak to my daughter sometime today. She called last night and asked if I'm going to do anything special tomorrow. I said, "Why? Mom's anniversary? That's not till the day after tomorrow."

She said, "No, it's tomorrow."

I said, "Sunday a week ago was Valentine's Day, so the fourteenth. So yesterday, Sunday, was the twenty-first. So today... you're right. The twenty-second. And tomorrow's the twenty-third. No, I'm not going to do anything. I used to light a memorial candle. But the last time, the flickering for twenty-four hours got to me. It was too much, like someone was in the room. The shadows on the wall. And I got worried, leaving the house, that the candle might fall out of the tuna fish can I had it standing up in."

"I can understand," she said.

"You going to do anything?" I said.

"No, just like you, she'll be on my mind a lot."

I go into the bedroom she died in. She's lying in bed, on her back, eyes open. She looks like she's been thinking. A poem, maybe, she's writing in her head.

"I had a dream of us last night," I say. "Actually, this morning. Didn't sleep well. But the dream was one of the best I've ever had of you. We were both being graduated from college. We were the ages we were when we met. Not kids in their early twenties. It was shortly after the graduation ceremony and you said you wanted me to meet your parents. You took my hand and brought me over to them. They were very short. Just an inch or two above five feet. And from Hungary, while yours were from Poland and Russia. And your father had a beard, something he never had. He shaved every day. He once told me that not a day had passed in sixty years when he hadn't shaved. Then you looked at me and we just sort of stood frozen and looked at each other and you said you'd never felt so close to someone by just looking into his eyes. I felt the same, I said in the dream. Then we took each other's hands and kissed in front of your dream parents. But such a deep, long kiss that we forgot—I know I did and I thought you did too—that we were around other people. Then your father in the dream, who still looked nothing like your father in real life, said we'll all meet tonight at a restaurant in Cuernavaca and it'd be his and your mother's treat. But that was such a real kiss. I mean, it felt so real, as satisfying as a real kiss. I felt your lips pressed to mine. Your lips were very soft. I can still feel them."

I lie down on the bed in the room she died in. Maybe lying on a different bed from the one I always sleep on will help me get to sleep and stay asleep awhile. I lie on my back, fold my hands together on my chest, shut my eyes, and try to sleep. I won't be able to work today, I feel so tired. My French friend died about six months ago. My daughter lives in Brooklyn and is working toward a doctorate in Russian literature at a university in Manhattan. She wants me to sell the house and buy a one-bedroom condominium in New York, Brooklyn or Manhattan. But everything is here for me. And for as long as I can continue to drive, everything is convenient for me. Doctors, dentist, shopping, the Y every day, an occasional concert or movie downtown. Everything is here except my daughter and a few old friends in New York. But mainly I don't want to go through the hassles of selling the house and getting rid of almost everything in it and looking for a condominium and wondering what to do about the car and moving to New York. And my cat spends half the day outdoors, it seems, when it isn't raining or snowing or icy cold, and I wouldn't want to deprive him of that. He'd go crazy, I think, after seven years of going outside whenever he wants to and there's still daylight. I'd feel bad for him. That might sound silly, but I would, and I'd never stop feeling bad for him.

I can't fall asleep. The mind, it just keeps going. I get off the bed. It was seven years ago today, in this room, and just around this time—8:45 a.m.—when she died and my French friend called from Paris. My daughter and I sat on either side of the bed till the hospice nurse came. That was around 10. She examined my wife, declared her dead, broke in two the morphine capsules that were left, called the hospice doctor to come over to fill out some forms. I called the funeral home to pick up her body for cremation. It had been prearranged and paid for a few days before. They knew she was coming, just not when. The van came. White; very clean, as if it had just been hosed down. No identifying markings on the outside of it. It could have been transporting anything. She was put in a body bag and wheeled out on a gurney. My daughter and I went out to watch the gurney get wheeled up a ramp into the van, strapped down, watched the rear doors close and the van drive away. We looked at each other, as if saying, *What are we going to do now?* She borrowed my car to meet her closest friend in town and I went to bed.

I get up and go into our bedroom. She's getting dressed. I say, "You look lovely today. You always look lovely, but for some reason more so today."

"You're so sweet," she says. She looks at me. Stares, as in the dream. I stare back at her, don't take my eyes off her face. We take each other's hands. Hold them as we were instructed to do by the rabbi at our wedding ceremony.

She says, "Strange, but I never felt so close to someone by just looking into that person's eyes."

"Me too," I say. "A very strange feeling came over me, looking at you."

"Me too," she says. "Let's kiss."

"You don't have to ask me twice," I say. We kiss. A long, deep one. Her lips have never felt so soft. I've never experienced a kiss like this in my life. I've had longer kisses with her and with other women. But none have ever been as deep. It lasts for about a minute. When it is over, I say, "I think I have to sit down."

I should shave, I think. I'll go into the bathroom and let the water run in the sink till it's warm. I'll take my razor and shaving soap and brush out of the medicine cabinet, splash warm water on my face, wet the brush, swish it around the shaving soap till I get a lather, and apply the brush to my face and start to shave.

THE PITCH

BY LAURA VAN DEN BERG

IN THE CHILDHOOD PHOTO my husband showed me, I noticed something strange. He had found the photo in a wood crate filled with his father's things. We had driven several such crates home with us after the funeral in Lake City, Florida, two weeks ago. In the picture, my husband was standing in the woods, shirtless and barefoot and holding a fishing rod. Thirteen years old, slender and pale, a streak of mud on his cheek, one of his father's too-big belts knotted around his waist. Americana all the way.

My husband's mother, I have been told, died in childbirth. When we first met, he'd had a nasty habit of leaving his dirty socks on the bathroom floor, and when I asked him, "Were you raised in the woods or what?" he replied, "As a matter of fact, I was."

The woods in the photo are called the Pitch, because the tree cover is so dense that not even the fabled Florida sunshine can blunt the shadows.

The first time my husband mentioned these woods—reachable on foot from his childhood home in northern Florida—I'd asked him if the name had something to do with baseball, and he'd said, "No, like pitch-dark," and then I'd said, "As in Renata Adler?" (I'd read her novels in college), and he'd looked at me like I was hopeless.

We went to the Pitch once and walked around in there, back when my husband's father was dying but not yet dead, and I'd wondered who is in charge of naming things, how such decisions are made.

I was fond of my father-in-law and had felt very sorry when he announced to us that he was dying, and remained sorry even when he began to flood my voicemail with messages, left in the middle of the night, during the last month of his life. During this time, I had tried to engage my husband on the subject of his impending orphanhood, but he'd refused. Instead he spent his free time cultivating his rose garden, examining the teas for signs of distress, and pruning his floribundas; he ordered expensive mulches online and frequented a nearby slaughterhouse for fresh manure. From the window of my backyard studio I had observed him bending over the wide faces of the floribundas and whispering to them; clearly, he regarded the roses as superior confidantes.

Yet I can't say that I was thinking about any of this when my husband showed me the photo. I was too busy looking at the boy in the background, small and white as milk and shimmying up a tree.

"Who's that?" I asked my husband, pressing my thumb over the boy's head. We were standing in my studio, just under a small skylight; I had been at work all day on an illustration project commissioned by a wealthy eccentric.

He snatched the photo from me. "What do you mean *who?* That's me. The man you married."

"Not *you*," I said, already exasperated. One unfortunate side effect of marriage was knowing the mistakes a person was going to make before they actually made them. I stood beside him and pointed at the boy in the tree.

He held the photo close to his face. He blinked like he had something in his eye. Had he really not noticed the boy until this very moment? It was summer in the picture, which meant everyone walked around looking like they'd just been sprayed with a hose, and yet my husband's skin was cool and dry.

"I see what you're seeing." He began to nod. "I didn't before, but now I do."

He explained that the boy was not a boy at all, but rather a large vine wrapped around the tree trunk, bleached and distorted by exposure. He pushed the photo under my nose.

"Whatever you say." I returned to my desk, pressed a pencil to my sketchpad. I could feel my husband hovering over me, could hear him saying my name, but I did not look up—not if he was going to try and tell me I had mistaken a vine for a boy. That may have been the story he was intent on telling himself, but I wasn't about to let it infect me; I didn't yet understand that refusing one kind of story can activate another.

You draw one line and then draw another, I told myself, until I heard the studio door open and close, felt the air settle.

The next thing I knew it was dusk and I was standing by the window, at a momentary loss for how to proceed with the next phase of my illustration project, and my husband was in the backyard with a grill light and a shovel. I watched him set the photograph on fire and then bury the ashes in the ground, a safe distance from the roses.

*   *   *

After the incident with the photo, my husband's every movement adopted an aura of menace. I would look up from my desk and see his face pressed to the window of my studio or turn from the kitchen sink and find him right behind me in socked feet, perched on his tiptoes like a gargoyle. He put his father's things on a high shelf in the garage, too high for me to reach, especially now that our ladder seemed to have gone missing. My husband worked as a receptionist for a psychiatrist, Dr. X, and began coming home late. From bed, I would hear the car rumble into the driveway, and once he was beside me I would, somewhat against my will, fall into a sleep so deep it was like being absorbed into a black hole, though I can't say that I ever felt "at rest." My husband continued to spend all his free time fussing over his roses. He started wearing his green gardening gloves indoors, leaving dirt trails on counters and side tables, charting his path through the house.

When he was around, he pestered me with strange questions. "Have you been checked for cataracts?" he asked one morning, peeling an orange with his gloved hands. "Have you ever suffered from psychodynamic visual hallucinations?" he asked on another.

"Is that something you heard from Dr. X?" I said back. "Do you even know what those words mean?" My husband had always called his employer Dr. X, and I had joined him in this practice because in a marriage few things are more powerful than shared habits. And then a few years ago we attended the office holiday party and I learned that everyone called him Dr. X—shorthand for a name, the doctor told me, that he had grown tired of people mispronouncing.

"I don't understand what the big commotion is all about," I said to my husband in our kitchen. "I saw what I saw, and I saw a boy in that tree."

I couldn't make sense of what was going on. My husband had never been the kind of person who demanded that everyone agree with his version of things, but perhaps he was turning into one. I told myself that he had been terribly unsettled by his father's death. I told myself that grief, especially when it was not properly tended to, could turn someone hostile and confused. Maybe he needed to make an appointment with Dr. X for himself instead of taking down the appointments of others; surely there was an employee discount.

I read up on double exposure and grief. I read up on spirit photography. I tried to understand why my husband would not, or could not, see the boy in the tree even after I had made his presence known. Had he truly been unable to see the boy, or had he been waiting for me to notice him all along? Had his not-seeing been a charade or some kind of test? From the library I checked out *Chronicles of the Photographs of Spiritual Beings and Phenomena Invisible to the Material Eye Interblended with Personal Narrative.* Yet nothing provided an explanation as satisfying as the one I knew to be true the moment I saw the photograph—my husband had done something to the boy in the tree.

A great many people know the name Margaret Wise Brown, but how about Clement Hurd, who illustrated *Goodnight Moon* and who studied with cubists in Paris? By the time my husband introduced his childhood photo into our lives, I'd had a very successful run of illustration projects, all with major publishers, though I had not won a Caldecott Medal.

The things that hadn't happened, the honors not bestowed, had never bothered me earlier in my career, when time felt like a field without a visible horizon—but now that dark line had appeared in the distance, and the story I had always told myself about my own limitless prospects was breaking down; *not yet* was starting to feel more like *not ever.*

That summer, the commission from the wealthy eccentric was my sole job. This happened on occasion, someone coming along with a vanity project and enough money to make it a real thing in the world. The author intended to self-publish the book, and when I received the text it was like no children's book I had ever seen—a story about a surrealist ballet troupe made up of animals. Later the reader learned the troupe was being held captive by a terrible dictator in an unnamed country. The animals, tired of dancing to *Ballet mécanique*, longed for escape. At the end, a giraffe made a run for it and was shot dead by a firing squad. The wealthy eccentric had suggested I watch Jean Cocteau's dadaist ballet *Les mariés de la Tour Eiffel* for inspiration. It was a bewildering experience. Halfway through, a lion galloped onto the stage and ate a dancer for breakfast.

I did not care for the ballet. The music set my nerves on edge—and I wasn't alone. When my husband heard *Les mariés de la Tour Eiffel* emanating from my studio one weekend, two weeks after he'd showed me the photo, he ran over and began pounding on the door. He was wearing his gardening gloves and brandishing a small pair of shears. His own long-dead mother had been a dancer as a young woman, though I had always imagined her doing classical productions like *The Nutcracker* or *Swan Lake.*

I put on my headphones and he retreated from the door. I sensed that his comprehension of the world around him was becoming constricted in a way I did not yet understand.

I wasn't sure if the wealthy eccentric's story was intended to be a comment on authoritarian regimes or the privatization of art or the cruelty of keeping animals in captivity. I truly I had no idea, though I felt certain no child would ever want to read it. To test my theory, I waited by the backyard fence until the neighbor's little boy came out to play.

"Have you ever heard of *Ballet mécanique* or *Les mariés de la Tour Eiffel?*" I asked the boy through the wood slats. "Do you know what a dictator is?"

The boy yelped and ran inside. Not long after, his mother called and demanded to know what was wrong with me, bringing up French words and dictators to an eight-year-old.

"You don't behave how people are supposed to," the mother huffed into the phone.

That night, as I ate dinner alone, standing at our kitchen island, I pictured my husband working after hours in Dr. X's office, filing paperwork in his gardening gloves.

Often children's book illustrators are expected to have whimsical natures—a foolish expectation, for all the best children's literature, if anyone has been paying attention, hinges on betrayal, the heartlessness of nature, death.

As it happened, my husband was adamantly against us having children, given what had happened to his own mother. He said that mothers terrified him and he would lose his mind if I ever became one. In the early years of our marriage, I'd had fantasies about testing the limits of his revulsion. If I handed him a forged pregnancy test, for example, would I turn fearsome and unrecognizable right before his eyes?

Despite the shortcomings of the wealthy eccentric's story, I had become quite fond of the animals themselves, given all the time I had spent coaxing them to life. To cope with the personal loss I anticipated feeling at the project's end, I decided to repaint the living room walls. I left paint samples scattered around the house, and when my husband was home, I made a big show of reviewing them, scrutinizing the difference between Shy Violet and Mountain Majesty. Really, though, the paint job was a cover-up for a secret plan.

First, I would cover the living room floor in plastic sheeting and haul all the furniture into the center. I estimated it would take me two days to paint the walls. Once the paint had dried, I planned to stencil a miniature version of each animal onto areas that would be covered once the furniture had been returned to its rightful place.

I was starting to feel like I was in need of reinforcements.

I never told my husband about the voicemails his dying father left me in the middle of the night. I suppose it was the way my father-in-law always called at a time when he knew he would not reach me and rambled on until my voicemail was full—the whole thing had the tone of a confessional.

In these messages, my father-in-law told me he had decided to limit his food intake to what was farmed in Florida, which amounted to consuming a great deal of citrus and sugarcane, sweet corn, and boiled peanuts. He had regular sexual fantasies about the woman in the red uniform who rang a bell for the Salvation Army outside Walmart. He told me he had visited Teotihuacán in the '60s—before he was married, before he was a father—and had saved a French tourist from leaping to her death from the top of the sun pyramid. She had climbed all the way up there to die. Many years would pass before he heard the phrase "suicide tourism"—which struck him as such a rude plan, to travel to a different country for the express purpose of making a bloody mess. My father-in-law said he'd grabbed this French tourist by the shoulders and shook her so hard her sunglasses fell off her face and clattered down the side of the pyramid. "Look at all this beauty," he'd said. To my voicemail he confessed that he wouldn't know what to tell a suicidal person now, as an older man, nor did he know what had happened to the French tourist after they got down from the pyramid. Yet this was the only time he could say with any certainty that he'd helped save a life.

I wondered if he'd held on to this fact so tightly because he'd been unable to save his own wife. They had been on their way to the hospital when the car broke down. She'd given birth on the side of the road and then bled out in the back seat. Umbilical cord cut with pliers.

His final message was just static and silence and then, right before the cutoff, he said: "Did I ever tell you about my other son?"

The first time I listened to the message, I felt like I was holding a cold stone in my mouth. After I played it again, I decided to chalk his words up to delirium; after all, being in close contact with the end of all time could make a person behave very strangely. But when my husband showed me the photo, with the pale boy perched in the tree—the boy my husband refused to recognize, the boy who compelled him to burn and bury the evidence—well, the memory returned like an avalanche.

Did I ever tell you about my other son?

I decided to put the question to my husband directly. One morning I poured him a coffee and pressed the mug into his gloved hands, the fingertips damp and dark from soil, and whispered, "Did I ever tell you about my other son?" By then my living room paint job was under way and the entire house reeked of chemicals. I wondered if the smell was making us both a little delirious.

He startled, sloshing coffee over the rim of the mug and onto the gleaming tips of his dress shoes. He began making wild accusations. He said that I didn't know what I was doing, that I was insisting on keeping a terrible story alive, and when I told him he wasn't making sense, he put the mug down on the kitchen island, hard enough to slosh more coffee, and fled our house through the garage.

I refilled his mug and dropped a couple of ice cubes in, because that was how I took my coffee in the summertime. I followed a faint dirt trail from the kitchen to the garage, where the door was raised; the driveway was empty. I stood barefoot on the cool stone floor, wondering what to do next. Already the ice had melted into translucent slivers. I stared up at the highest shelves, searching for a way to climb up and see what else could be discovered among my father-in-law's things, and that was when I realized that all the boxes were gone.

That night my husband did not come home. When he turned up the following day, he claimed he had fallen asleep at the office, but he did the same thing the next night, and before long he was coming home only to shower and change; he claimed Dr. X had never been so busy. I would watch him struggle to peel a banana in his gardening gloves and wonder how long it would take for his beloved roses to wither from inattention.

Alone more than usual, I was productive. I submitted my illustrations to the wealthy eccentric and then called her up, under the guise of wanting to ensure that my work was satisfactory. Really, though, I longed to ask why she had written the book in the first place. Did she have a particular child in mind for this story, and, if so, was this child perhaps a bit *unusual*? She explained that she had not written the book for a child at all; rather, the story was translated directly from a dream that had been plaguing her for years. Sometimes she was the bear. Sometimes she was the giraffe. Always she was the animal that attempted to flee and that was shot dead on sight; she never learned her lesson. She thought that if she made the dream real, it would lose its power over her.

"But I'm starting to think," she said before we got off the phone, "that I might have made a terrible mistake."

A few weeks later, after the paint dried, I spent two afternoons stenciling animals on the walls: a galloping giraffe behind the TV, a bear in a tutu on a patch that would be hidden by a corduroy armchair. Our living room was now their habitat. I made the bear look gentle and entreating—head tilted, one front paw raised—even though I knew it stood ready to rip out someone's throat. When my drawings were finished, I pushed all the furniture back into place.

"You can never be too careful," I said to the whiskered lion peeking out from behind the ball-shaped lampshade. "You can never be too sure."

I was about to start rolling up the plastic sheeting when I heard a car rumble into the driveway, and then my husband was standing on the edge of the living room, holding a large cardboard book. I watched him survey the walls, now painted a color called Suave Mauve.

"You're home," I said, wiping sweat from my forehead.

"Seems so." He set the box down on the plastic sheeting. He pulled up at the edges of his gardening gloves, sinking his fingers deeper into the fabric.

"You've been working so hard," he said next. He rubbed the sheeting with the toe of his dress shoe. "Why don't you lie down?"

"Don't be sinister," I said. "What would Dr. X say?"

"Dr. X sent me away. He said that I was developing a filing compulsion and needed to take a vacation."

"Good," I said, nodding. "We can take one together."

"I did everything I could," he said back, and his entire body seemed to deflate a little.

I told my husband that I had no idea what he was talking about and that, in fact, I hadn't had any idea what he was talking about for some time now. In response, he brandished his car keys and sliced open the box, revealing a row of book spines. The wealthy eccentric had sent me copies. I went over to him and lifted one from the box. I turned the pages, showing my husband my fine drawings of the animals dancing the *Ballet mécanique.*

When I got to the illustration of the firing squad taking aim at the giraffe, he pulled the book from my hands. He got down on one knee like he was proposing (when he'd asked me, years ago, we were in a swimming pool and we both came up for air at the same time, our faces shiny with water, and then he said, "How would you feel about doing this for the rest of your life?"). I slipped off his gardening gloves, one at a time; his skin was soft and pale from the lack of sunlight, his fingertips a bit pruned.

"I'm serious about that vacation," I said to him. "We could leave right now. We could go kayaking with manatees. We could go to the beach."

He squeezed my hands and asked if I wanted to drive out to the Pitch.

Behind the furniture the animals snorted and stomped.

I was raised in the desert and had always appreciated the way its landscape gives you a chance to see what's coming. In Florida, dangers don't reveal themselves until it's too late. The alligator lurking in the shallow pond, ready to devour your pet or your child. The snake hidden in the underbrush. The riptide slicing across that postcard-perfect Atlantic. Sinkholes. Encephalitis. Brain-destroying bacteria that flourish in overheated lakes. Quicksand.

In the car, my husband said that lately he had been thinking about his childhood in Sanderson, Florida—about the things that had happened there. He had tried to stop doing so, but found that he was unable; before he sent my husband home, Dr. X had told him that that which could not be forgotten must be confronted. I stared down the endless gray line of the highway. The sky was clear; I felt the sunshine in my lungs. My husband's hands gleamed on the steering wheel.

At the Pitch, I followed him out into a sea of darkening green. I ducked under ropes of moss and mildewed branches. I kept my eyes on my feet. I took high, careful steps.

"Do I know everything about you?" my husband asked as we walked.

"Everything except my thoughts."

We went on for a while in silence, twigs snapping under our feet. I considered the possibility that our thoughts were the most important thing to know, because they made up the stories we told ourselves about the world and our place in it, what was possible and what was sacred and what was forbidden.

"Also," I added, "your father left me voicemails in the middle of the night when he was dying."

Ahead I watched my husband nod, as though he had all along suspected some kind of treasonous communication between his father and me.

"He told me all kinds of things," I added.

My husband swatted away a branch. "Did he, now."

I relayed the stories about the sexual fantasies about the woman from the Salvation Army, about the French tourist from Teotihuacán and how he had saved her life with beauty. I was surprised by how much I had to say.

"My father did not have the first idea about how to save a life," my husband said. His steps turned long and quick across the forest floor.

"Did I ever tell you about my other son?" I pressed. I thought it might be worth putting the question to him again in the outdoors, even as I sensed us skittering toward a place from which we would not easily return. "That's what he said to me, in his last message. He said that and then he died."

My husband stopped in front of a tree. A massive water hickory, with a gnarled, mossy trunk and powerful roots, arranged in a way that resembled the giant hands of a pianist: fingers suspended above the keys, curled in anticipation. I touched the trunk and was surprised at how warm and supple the wood felt, almost like skin. Something about this tree was terribly familiar.

"That photo I showed you was taken by our father," my husband said. "A month before my brother disappeared."

He told me that the first time he and his brother heard their mother's voice in the Pitch, they told themselves it was just the wind. They told themselves it was their own sadness. Their mother, though—she was persistent. *Little boys kill things and climb trees.* His brother started climbing tree after tree, determined to root out the source of the voice, and then one day he went up into this very tree and never came back down.

A police report was filed. A search party combed the woods. My father-in-law hadn't believed my husband's explanation of what happened. He suspected my husband had done something to his brother, disappeared him on accident or on purpose, and since he was not prepared to lose another child, he decided they would simply never speak of the missing one again.

As I listened to my husband, all these years later, I wasn't sure what or whom to believe. Conveniently, he was the only survivor, leaving no one to contradict his story. My sneakers sank down into the forest muck. I looked around for a big stick that I could pick up in a hurry.

It took a long time for him to forget about his brother, but eventually he did. Or maybe *forget* was not the right word. His memory was like a faint scuttling beneath the floorboards of a house. It was like eating a sumptuous meal to the barely audible sound of animals being slaughtered in the backyard. He had worked very hard to convince himself that there had never been a brother at all, that his brother's short life had been nothing but a strange and persistent dream, and he thought he had succeeded in getting the story of his brother to turn dormant—that is, until I looked at the photo and sought out the little boy in the tree.

"Maybe if you weren't so ruthless." My husband wrung his gleaming hands. "Maybe then we wouldn't be out here."

I thought it was unfair of my husband to blame *me* for the bizarre state in which we currently found ourselves, but I kept that to myself. I did not have a good feeling about where we were heading. I spotted a stick the size of a club near my feet. I picked it up and held it like a batter on a mound.

He removed his tie and stepped out of his shoes. He cuffed his shirtsleeves.

I can still scarcely believe what happened next, and maybe I shouldn't, and maybe you shouldn't, either, not with the way I was waving that big stick around as my husband called me ruthless. Who was *I* to be trusted?

But I'll tell you anyway.

Right when I was thinking I might drop the stick and reach for him, to say that everything was going to be all right and he would make it through this thicket of grief, or at least make a case for it being too early in our marriage to seriously consider murder, he slung his arms and legs around the tree trunk. He began to climb fast toward the top. I yanked the bottom of his pant leg; he shook me off. I ran circles around the base like an agitated dog, yelping his name. I tried to climb after him, but kept sliding down the trunk—and the moment I found a nub to rest my foot on, something to help propel me up the tree, an inner voice commanded: *Stop.* So I stood back, watched his white hands clutch and claw. I watched his toes find the wood knots, points on a map he'd never forgotten. Once he was in the dark bramble of the canopy, his body vanished. I waited for a long time, long past nightfall, but he never came down.

I walked out of the Pitch and, in the years that followed, wrote and illustrated a book about a little boy whose dead mother communicates with him through a tree in the woods behind their house. She tells her sad son wise and soothing things. The book was a great success. Very popular with the newly grieving. *This is a gentle lie*, I did not tell the half-orphaned children in signing lines. *This tree wants nothing more than to destroy your life.* I marveled at the story I had gotten so many people to believe. And then one day I got a call from a number in New York City—at long last, I was told, I had won my prize.

COUP DE THÉÂTRE

BY GORDON LISH

WHEN I WAS IN primary school, or is it that it was in grammar school
that I was in, more exactly, more on-the-nose-ish-ly, in the eighth grade
thereof, I performed the role of Rafe in the Gilbert and Sullivan operetta
H.M.S. Pinafore.

Sylvia Wachsburger played the part of the captain's daughter, and
Janice Birnbaum played the part of Buttercup, and I, Gordon, took
myself, not as Rafe the tar but as Gordo the star, to be beauteously
maddened out of my tree for both of them, but marked, however, by
such an abundance of lucklessness as to bar me forever from my ever
once savoring the seasoning reaching my clichéd senses from the newly
christened crotches of my co-religionists, there in the blazing ravel-
ment of their thespian allure. Thus it was with doubled piquance that
I, Gordon—Gordo!—flared my nostrils and proposed to the rabble

assembled in the school's assembly hall the song of my ravishing heart-break of stage-craftedly shocked resignation.

Farewell, my own, light of my life, farewell—for crimes unknown I go to my dungeon cell.

I sang not to Wachsburger nor to Birnbaum, but with all my deceit to naught but the parents and teachers.

Unless it was to the teachers and parents that I sang.

It was long ago.

Thus.

Oh, hark!

Oh, harken!

I ask for no more than that you please just listen.

Farewell, my own, light of my life, farewell—for crimes unknown I go to my dungeon cell.

You heard every word?

Attenday every word?

Farewell, my own, light of my life, farewell—

I was what?

Was I all yet of not even a teen yet but was still, may non, only all of twelve years old? Think of it!—at most not even one year more than only twelve years old, yet already reckoning so ruefully in the matter of life and amour.

Unless I have just spelt it wrong.

Have I just spelt everything wrong?

O Jan!

O Syl!

Yesterday the age I turned when I turned yesterday the older age I am—oh, hear me, help me!—it was yesterday eighty-four that I just yesterday turned!

O Burger!

O Baum!

Listen, I implore you for you to just to please for just this once this one more time to please for you to please for the mercy of God to please be so good as to maybe really this one last time please actually really and truly listen.

Farewell, my own, light of my life, farewell—for crimes unknown I go to my dungeon cell.

Unless it's he goes.

Is it he who goes?

Or went?

Unless it is he who goes is what the chorus sings.

Like, you know, litaneutically?

Anyway, that was theatre for me. And music for me. And amour for me. And now I am eighty-four years old, and all there is that is left for me is me.

And Percy Bysshe Shelley.

A BRIEF HISTORY
OF GROCERY STORES

BY T KIRA MADDEN

WE SQUINTED OUR WAY through yellow lights, kiss-kissing the roof for luck, speeding. Most grocery stores close at 9:00 p.m. out west; did you know that? We had traveled so far—five days of dry mouth and road ache and the Ronettes and Styrofoam coffee cups—and we had made it: Blinky's, just before close. Yes, we would have breakfast the next morning in a *home*, not a motel room. We'd have sex on a dining room table, soap each other's bodies in somebody else's shower. We would clear the pipes, muck the stalls. Fuck again against the barn door.

We'd come in a used pickup truck we bought for five hundred dollars. Red. Our bags slung in back, bungee cords choking our blankets, our duffels full of blue jeans and paddock boots, cassette tapes, rubber cocks. Eight fifty p.m. in a town we didn't know. We were headed to that little brick house, borrowed, one we hoped to buy in a few months' time. For now, we were taking care. Clearing the pipes, mucking the stalls of the animals out back. That's what we were told, anyway. That's how we were instructed. We never did get there.

That grocery store light still on. The sliding doors, clenching.

Oh, we felt so fucking lucky.

The universe will put you exactly where you need to be, exactly when. I said that. I'm lying. You did.

We parked the truck around the side of the building, in the dark. All of our possessions in back. *Who would want to steal this crap, anyway?* Because really we had left so much back home; we were starting over, you and I, without our velvet Elvis painting or my box of childhood teeth, cobalt vases, your old ukulele. We had only exactly what was needed. Still, we were careful.

We locked the doors when we hopped out. I remember that part. That manual lock that kept sticking; I pushed it down like I was trying to drown it. We clicked a dial clockwise to turn the truck lights off. You did that. Neither one of us remembered it.

Our bags. We checked them, made sure they hadn't tumbled off the truck bed. We'd situated cinder blocks around them in a square to keep them secure; I don't know what it is we were checking. The bags could not fly off without our noticing. Bags cannot misbehave. I think we were checking just to check. Maybe because we'd never had any children.

We squeezed hands as we walked around the building to the entrance.

The country bugs sounded almost percussive.

Feels so good to stretch out, I said, kissing you on the temple.

Inside Blinky's, we dropped hands. Of course we did. Desire, for people like us, should not—could not—be held up to the light.

You grabbed the cart, detaching it from the long row of them. It spangled there, under the bulbs. I placed my purse inside. Leather, bruised thing, stretched at the straps. Another thing that was once my mother's. I would never have carried a purse if it weren't for that.

Where to start? you said. You never cooked; you didn't know your way around a grocery store. Your hair looked green in the light. Maybe it was a special effect of the eye—pinwheel hours of night road adjusting to fluorescents.

That frittata. I'd made it the first week we met. You, in airport security; you in your creased blue uniform. I'd just flown six hours from back home, wearing the ripe look of death. You helped me lift a suitcase, remembered me from weeks before. It was late. Your shift was ending. You came back to my apartment and never left.

Pretty friend you have, said my neighbor. *She moving in?*

I think he wanted you. Everybody has always wanted you. That's your curse.

When I cooked this for you for the first time, you pierced the surface with your fork, let the balloon of egg collapse into a stream of fat smoke, said something like *You taste like home.*

I'm lying again. You wouldn't say that. You are simpler in your love. You ate it, scraped your plate, nothing more to it.

You never even flew on a plane.

Did you know I haven't eaten an egg since Blinky's, since that night? Eggs are a difficult food to avoid. Outside of breakfast preparations, they are a necessary ingredient in breads, pastries, salad dressings, pastas, fried foods, cakes baked for celebrations.

Frittata—how innocuous. Lazy, even. Nothing sexy about it.

Inside, next to the vegetables, my shoulders chilled. You pumped your hands up and down my bare arms like you were sanding something. Around the aisles we went. It was closing soon. We moved quickly. At one point, I stood on the front edge of the cart and let you push me. *Brace yourself*, you said, as you jerked the cart, cut corners, trying to throw me like a steed.

You need a workout, cowgirl. We laughed. Maybe I stepped off and kissed you because nobody was around. Probably not. I'm getting distracted.

The Gruyère cheese. It wasn't where it should have been. It wasn't in the dairy aisle, near the yogurts, the other cheeses. I scanned every label twice. That fancier cheese; it wasn't there.

Let's split up. It's closing soon. You said that.

No, I did.

We did split up. You went to find the baking soda, paper goods, maybe sweets. You went to find essentials, foods that would keep us happy for the next week or so. I stayed there facing that chilled silver glow and counting that list of ingredients in my head and you went away. You took the cart.

I don't remember the last thing we said to each other before you did that.

Maybe it was about the fact that we were hungry, or the fact that we would wake up tomorrow in a place we could share, no one for miles, at last. I was right about this move; things would be different now. We liked facts; repeating them until they went true.

I stood dumbly in front of those cheeses. I repeated their labels again. Parmesan, pecorino, ricotta, every shade of cheddar. I read them aloud to myself.

I read them, back and forth. You see, I was incredibly focused.

That's how I missed the announcement.

Did you know: the average grocery store has nineteen aisles. The average grocery store is forty-five thousand square feet, carrying an average of 42,200 items. The average person spends forty-one minutes inside a grocery store, per visit, if they shop beyond the outer perimeter. We stayed for only half of that.

At some point, I gave up on my aisle. I walked toward the other side of the store. The Gruyère could be by the bread, the deli. The made-to-order sandwich area. Maybe. Midway through the store, I stopped at the bathroom. I squatted over the dank seat and pissed a color too dark from all the road coffee. The tiles shone wet with something. They sucked at the bottom of my boots.

I imagine it was then, while I was squatting, pissing, kicking the flusher, that you went outside.

Why did you go?

I scrubbed my hands with a sour cherry soap. The tacky film of it stayed between my fingers; I felt it for days. Then I went on walking to that deli section. I turned my head left to look for you in every remaining aisle until I got there. My head ticked like a projector, but all the aisles were clear, bright, empty.

The deli section had its own refrigerator, long and opened like a coffin in the center of it all. We had missed it before. There they were, the fancy cheeses, facing the hunks of meat, the hams wrapped in fishnets.

There it was. The Gruyère. If only one of us had thought of it—the deli area—first.

On average, thirty-two million Americans visit a grocery store every day. Most of them bring a list. Most of them shop alone.

Inside of those minutes, from the moment you walked off with the cart to the moment I found the cheese, here is what I heard: refrigerators humming on and off; Patsy Cline, muddled, metallic, as if her voice had been forced through a sieve inside of that speaker system; the clanging of a few final carts and loose wheels weaving around the two registers; the unbearably quiet patters of rubber soles against tile, pushing.

I didn't hear the announcement.

What label was I reading when the announcement came? What was I thinking about when the speaker said, *To the red Ford pickup: you've left your lights on?* Was I dreaming into something else? Or more present than that?

Why did you go? It was closing so soon. We were almost done.

Perhaps because you said that truck was a junk piece of equipment. Because we'd had to check the oil three times between Texarkana and Abilene. Because it sputtered and changed gears for no reason, and the seats were perforated with burn marks, and the door handle was really just the strap of a seat belt stapled onto the door, and *This truck is too gross to even fuck in. I'm gonna catch a disease,* and the lock, well, it was always stuck.

I guess that's why the lights concerned you.

We were so close to our new home. The truck had been wheezing for days. You didn't want it to die.

I took four plastic-wrapped chunks of that cheese. They gleamed. I wanted to tear one open with my teeth and take a bite, but I didn't. We'd be unlocking our front door soon.

I carried two cheeses in each hand as I walked back toward the dairy aisle, where you'd left me. *Tick-tick* went my head again, every aisle.

Did you know that when I was a child, I always feared I'd lose my mother in a grocery store? She'd always send me on some task. Find the cereal, a sack of walnuts, the bananas, a waxy wrapped log of salami for my father. I'd find whichever item I'd been assigned, scan the alternatives—*snatch the cheapest, never the best*—and then I'd walk back and forth, back and forth, passing each aisle—*tick-tick*—looking for her. Somehow, she always managed to be walking between the aisles at the exact second that I stared my way through to the other side. Our timing was always like that, me and my mother. I'd cross back and forth through that store, convinced she had disappeared, shot off to Vegas with my father to live a life with sweating glasses, green casino tables, no accidental daughter, but she hadn't. She was always there.

Where were you? she'd say. *You're late.*

She was there.

Where the hell have you been?

You weren't.

You see, I have a history here.

A brief history of grocery stores.

I must have passed our cart on my way to the dairy aisle to look for you.

Our cart with every ingredient—the basil, the tomatoes, the rosemary, a whole carton of eggs—my mother's beaten purse.

I was looking for you. I wasn't going to stop. My head went *tick-tick* as I curled around, through the dairy aisle, to the back of the store. I passed the bathroom again, came back the other way. A grocery store is repetitive. In order to collect ingredients for the perfect meal, one must circle many times around. Nobody is an expert.

I crossed back. And then forth. Circled. The store was closing. An announcement told me that.

I heard that one.

Please check out, it said. *We are closing.*

What aisle was I on, what number was I counting, how hungry was I when they took you by the hair on that shadowed side of the building, the side that we'd called *safer?*

Your hair was ripped from the scalp, that's how I know.

What color did your hair look in the dark?

I began making my way through each aisle rather than passing them, as if you would spring out from the stacked cans of corn, manifest in the neat rows of paper towels. As if I had missed something.

My arms were cold. I stroked them myself.

At some point I called your name, embarrassed, then a little louder. No one answered.

I used to call *Mom!* when I was a child. Many moms answered, but never mine.

I made my way back to the registers. Perhaps, I thought, you wanted to begin checking out. You wouldn't keep employees waiting like that, after hours. They had lives to attend to, children and half-dashed crossword puzzles at home. You were always thoughtful like that. You ate quickly in restaurants when you saw other parties waiting for a table.

The registers were empty. Only one cashier working by then, another person at a customer-service desk stocked with magazines, cigarettes. It was there that I saw it.

The cart.

I approached it. Everything was still there, neatly inside. You had found the small can of baking soda. You had added a bag of apples. Why? I dropped the four cheeses into the cart, a slight bounce to them.

We're 'bout closed by now, said the woman at the customer-service desk.

Her face was shaded with a neatly shaved stubble the blue of skim milk. She wore a stained apron, a tag that read BONNIE.

You gotta git.

I'm looking for my friend, I said.

No specifics. I knew better.

She was pushing this cart, right here. I squeezed my fingers around the cart handle. I swear the plastic still felt warm.

Oh, yer friend, said Bonnie. Bonnie plucked a soft pack of Merits from the wall, tucking it into the front pocket of her apron. *Yeah, she was here.* Her eyes stayed focused on her front pocket, her chin down, creasing.

Well, when?

I made an announcement, said Bonnie. *Fella came inside and tells me your lights was on.*

I gotta close the register, she said.

So my friend, she went outside?

A nod.

So you gon' check out or what? she asked.

You were outside, waiting in the truck. You must be, I thought. You twisted that bag of apples, dropped them into the cart. You heard the announcement. You went outside, walked around to the dark side of the building, saw the yellow of our headlights glowing jagged up the trees like a crown. You took that steep step up into the truck and flicked the lights off. Outside the window, you saw the shadow of the man who had told Bonnie about the lights, and you cranked the window down to shout *Thank you, sir,* before he tipped his hat in your direction, *Sure thing.* A nice new town, you thought—what kindness. Maybe you started the car. The heat in our truck worked even though the air did not, and it was cool outside by now; we were so close to mountains. You decided to wait there for me, in the warm cabin of our shit truck. You'd forgotten your wallet, after all, and I had my purse. I could finish the job with the groceries. Yes, you were taking the time to spread out our maps, highlight the miles we had left, windy roads on a bleached landscape like hair on a bar of soap. You lit a cigarette and let the filter dangle. You drove the truck around to the front of the store, where you would be waiting when I stepped out the exit doors, grocery bags twisted around my wrists, spinning.

Maybe I did believe that.

I don't know.

What I mean to say is, I didn't go outside just then.

I let Bonnie do her job. I paid for my items. I didn't want to keep her waiting.

The universe will put you exactly where you need to be, exactly when.

She walked me to the other register. She needed the scale, she said, to weigh the apples. The other cashier was already closed out.

Patsy Cline was still warbling through the speakers. A whole album, I thought. How nice. If you screamed, this is why I didn't hear you.

I placed each item onto the flat black rubber.

I'm so sorry to keep you, I said, but Bonnie did not respond.

She smacked buttons and let the items roll, a red laser blinking beneath their stickers.

Our first breakfast together. Our new home. Look, every ingredient.

I reached into my mother's purse and took out my wallet. I scanned my credit card once, twice, *Please call your bank*. I apologized. *It's because I'm traveling*, I said. *The bank—they don't know.*

I found another credit card. The red one with a strip scratched as a matchbook.

Bonnie manually typed in the numbers, the zip code that was no longer mine.

This must have cost me another minute or two.

I took the plastic bags and let them catch on my wrists. I twisted them there, circled my hands around, like I always do. I like to feel my hands throb. I like them to purple, prickle on and off. I wished Bonnie a pleasant night.

What were the apples for? I had never seen you eat even one.

I let Patsy Cline fade out as I walked toward the exit, let the black-eyed sensor find me, open the automatic doors, a cool breeze rushing at me from both sides.

You weren't right there in our truck, waiting. It was quiet outside. It was slightly wet. Droplets fizzed around the parking lot lights like the surface of a soda. I looked left, and then right. *Tick-tick.* The bags spun as I made my way around the corner, to the safer side, that dark belt of asphalt and trees.

The truck lights weren't on. Of course they weren't.

You had turned them off, remember?

How could I have known, when I saw your legs dangling out the back of the truck, your jeans scrunched around your knees like the paper wrappers of two straws? One white sneaker on the ground, the glow of one bare foot; it's true that you never wore socks while long-distance driving—you liked to feel the pedals on your feet. How could I have known what they wanted to do to you, three sets of boot prints total? And why had we used cinder blocks anyway? Our bags were never going to cut loose, fly away. We should have trusted our things to stay put. The cinder blocks, stained wet-black. Oozing split where your hair should have been.

How could I have known?

I should have.

You knew my purse was in our cart. You would never have left it for long. You would never have kept me looking for you, waiting.

I knew that.

Hindsight is the opposite of gut. I once said that.

The eggs smashed exactly where I dropped them. My hands burned as the blood drained back. I used them to turn you over. I used them to touch what was left of your face, the parts that have scarred over into bright webs by now.

I used my hands to shake you. To love you.

You said that.

That my love brought you back. You could hear me somewhere, screaming.

I'm lying again.

I was late. I'm sorry. I have a history with these things.

How long did it take me to leave you? To run back inside to find Bonnie? To find a phone? What could have been saved in that time? Did you know I was gone, miss me?

Bonnie didn't remember the man, or what he wore, or the way he smelled, or anything about him. *He was very concerned*, she said, *about those lights.* That's what she told the police once they arrived.

And what's your relationship to the girl?

She's my friend, I said, *my very best friend.*

You see, I wanted them to help us.

The man had not been a customer. Bonnie knew that. He'd come inside from the parking lot, *out of the blue*. I'd held your hand in that parking lot before dropping it. I'd kissed you. I wasn't thinking. It was dark.

And you're sure you didn't leave the lights on?

We never made it, that's true. We didn't clear the pipes, muck the stalls. You never fucked the life back into my body. I never made that frittata.

We came back east, where it took you weeks, months, to arrange syllables. You remembered, but you didn't. Your words gurgled out like a clogged drain. Drool dragged from your lips.

I said, *Once, we were happy.*

Then, *My mother would have liked you.*

Your hair grew back jagged, in chunks. A rusty color in some places. Looking at it made me sick. You never flew on planes, because it wasn't safe. You'd been around enough to know.

How long did it take me to leave you? Again?

Lately, I can only swallow with my eyes closed.

THE FIELDS

BY COLIN WINNETTE

I WENT TO WORK in the fields where it was said people often find themselves. I blistered my first month or two, then I stopped. We were given one cup of coffee each in the morning, but I'm sure we would have been allowed to drink more than one cup if we could have found the time and the coffee, which I was never able to do. I woke up long before the sun most days, and enjoyed that part the most. It was like stepping into a layer of dust and letting it settle. Before all this, I was involved in something like college. When other people tell stories from college, it all seems very familiar. Like, I get the jokes. In the evenings, in the fields, we drank a clear elixir that sometimes made me feel like the fields were on fire. My friend/brother/cousin would hold my head and tell me the fields were not on fire just yet. Then some mornings the sun did not come up, or it was dark and gray the entire day, and they flooded the fields with artificial light. I could not make out the source of the light because it was so bright and high above me. I looked but never saw anything except for more light. Every now and then we found maggots/worms/caterpillars/spiders adhered to the underside of a cabbage. I sometimes ate the cabbage, which was very unpleasant against my teeth. And it gave me gas. I had to dig little holes in the rows of the fields. I wiped myself with the gray sleeves gathered around the broken heads we'd severed. The other workers moved right past me. Each person was on their own. There was a fight between two women one morning, and no one broke it up or said anything about it. We just moved right past them, and the noise died down. In the evening one of the women was bleeding from a small tear in her earlobe. The other woman was nowhere to be found. I can't understand fights, because I've only ever been able to run. The fear is that they will all one day catch up with me. We were sometimes fed in the evenings, chicken and rice and even old fish. We were given tiny desserts on little tin plates. Sometimes they were dried cakes and other times it was a kind of custard shaped into a circle and smothered with a sugary glaze. I do not remember liking dessert before I went to the fields, but while I was in the fields I did enjoy anything sweet that found its way to me. We all tried eating insects at one time or another. The most unpleasant part was putting the thing in your mouth and biting down. Everything after that—the texture, the taste, the wriggling, its going down, the digesting—those moments were unremarkable. What we were doing there was "clearing the cabbage." Those are the words I learned for the job. We prepared it to be picked by those who would come later. We would dislocate it, peel back the dressing, and set it aside to be gathered. We slept on thin mats in tents that sat in the dirt. It was comfortable enough to get to sleep when we were tired, and we were always tired. I'd had some trouble sleeping when I was still whoever I had been before I arrived, but I got over that in the fields. After enough time, I would sleep whenever I could, and I started having very long and detailed dreams that were difficult to interrupt and rise from to go about my work. The details came primarily from my days in the fields, but things were less difficult and a little more stunning to behold. Once, I was on an unruly horse that bucked me backward, then turned into a fox hiding among the leaves. I knew that if I chased it, it would get away. I realized that if I'd known that earlier, it wouldn't have been able to buck me. I did not spend a lot of time thinking about how good-looking things were in the fields, even if they were perfect for a painting by someone with talent. Someone with more time on their hands might have noticed how dull the sunlight was, how sharp the gray shades of the cabbage in its sleeve. It reminded me of California, of sunsets I'd seen there, or of clay cliffs in Massachusetts. The fields might even have been in California or Massachusetts but I could not say either and be 100 percent sure it was true. I was in a van for days is all I know, and then I was in the fields. I'd thrown up into a black baseball cap someone had curled deep into a cup holder. I couldn't remember any other time such a thing had happened to me. You lose bits and pieces as you go. When you see how much you can do with whatever sticks around, you realize just how little you really need to get by. Or maybe you don't lose anything at all. Maybe there's only ever more, and it's too hard to keep track of it all, eventually. I used to draw pictures of whatever I could remember at the end of each day in the fields, and these were truly disorienting things to look at. Monstrous in how far they seemed from what was in front of me when I woke. Some people seemed to like my drawings, but I never knew these people well. They did not give their names. They were not friendly, from what I can remember. They just came over and took a look. They wore dark clothing. They did not smile. They looked through my pictures and told me they were nice, honest, and skilled. They sometimes paid me for them, often in bills that were too crisp to be real. They sometimes paid me for drawings they claimed to have taken from me months before. "I've been meaning to get this to you," they would say, and they would hand me a curl of cash in a rubber band. I squirreled away the money. I hid it because I had no use for it, but someone else was likely to want it. We were fed. We had a place to sleep. But people always want more. The work we did in the fields had value, but we never saw the money. It went from people we did not know to others we had never met, and we were given the receipts. I did not try to leave. If I had, it could have happened very easily, or it could have gone very badly. I'm not sure. It's too dangerous to get to the bottom of anything. Here is what I know: I am not so different from a cabbage. I was blue and sheathed for years. Now I'm dislocated and raw. I think about what would happen if I sat in a field until something came to get me, and I realize that what would come to get me is the birds. Black birds are always hanging in the air, waiting for you to sit in the field until something comes to get you. It is what they live for. If they're lucky, they find a wire for a bit. They take a break. I broke my thumb with a rock so I might get closer to a woman with a bloody earlobe. I brought her some old drawings, and a few thoughts about birds, and my broken thumb to show her. She was sawing the husk of a cabbage, twisting it like the neck of an enemy soldier, and I realized I hadn't worked in days. I'd just been wandering the fields and trying to make a new drawing, but nothing new would come to me. I was losing weight. She didn't speak the language I spoke, but when I showed her my thumb she tilted her ear toward me to show me I was not alone. Hearing her speak, I realized all I'd ever done was make sound and draw pictures and break cabbage from its trap and chase women. I was skinny enough to be on the cover of a magazine, or on the cover of a book about workers in the fields. The next time I drank the clear elixir, a husband came to see me. He had a ring and a fist and a belt. The next day, I was able to work again. Or maybe it was a week after that. I was recommitted, and I cut the cabbage until I might have guessed that every cabbage in the world had been cut. It was a matter of discipline. When I felt finished, I looked back to see what I'd left in my wake. The gatherers had arrived. They were throwing heads into the back of a yellow truck. From the broken necks of the cabbage sprang more cabbage, and I painted my face with rust from the yellow truck to let them know I wasn't ready to commit. I dug into the old necks of the new cabbage until the truck couldn't carry any more loads. Until the tires popped from all I'd given it, and the truck grew into the dirt like a melon. Finally, I could sleep again. I tried to go as flat as I could get on a new cot I was given by the committee. It was just above the dirt. Off by only an inch or so. My drawings came back, and they were very dark during this time. I checked a coffee can I'd buried and found it full of money. More money than I could have known what to do with. I gave it to a kid who was still stuck in the truck, and he was happy to hold on to it, thinking it was coffee. He'd been left there, with the dirt growing over his broken yellow shell, and needed something to carry him through. He was mostly interested in trying to explain to me that he was inside of something that was outside, until the day he wasn't there anymore and there was just a mound of dirt where his voice had been. *Despair* is a word that holds the phrase "desperate for air" in its teeth. Your guts start to rot when you eat too much cabbage. Everyone in the fields was rotting and working. I was so thin now you could have snapped me into bits. You could liberate an appendage like a cabbage from its neck. I'd worn a chain necklace at one point, something a stranger I'd lived with in an apartment in a city far away had given to me. I'd worn it until it slid over my shoulders and down my arms, into the dirt. The dirt was always growing over something, and there were also floods coming. An earthquake had already started. That's how I noticed it: after the fact. I used to have this person in my life, an older woman, who was very concerned with kindness. I kept thinking about what that was worth when the volcanoes finally erupted. They had always been there, but a volcano is nothing more than a mountain until it opens up to you. The wind/ the water/the fire/the beasts that lived in the hills around us came pouring down one evening as plainly as a breath. Enemies we didn't even know were there, because enemies have nothing to do with cabbage. The fields were just an area where they'd drawn a long square, but beneath us you could find the ash of countless cities. You would think you'd have been able to hear some of the voices, but you absolutely could not. Death, death, death, lined up like heads of cabbage in a row. All I've ever learned is the way a lesson looks. For example, my broken thumb stopped screaming when a new nail crawled over the cracked one. Everything in a dangerous place is mute and worth your time.

CROWDED FIELDS

PHOTOS BY PELLE CASS

A
NATION OF LAWS,
A PEOPLE OF
COMPASSION

NONFICTION BY JOSÉ ORDUÑA

Tell us what they're looking at that gives them any hope.[1] —Lester Holt

I.

TRUMP INTERNATIONAL HOTEL SITS dead center on the horizon as you drive toward the Las Vegas Strip on Interstate 15—a silent, golden monument to the decay produced by our late-capitalist state. The pink and blood-orange reflection of the evening sky on its facade makes it look

---

1. Late into the night on November 8, 2016, John Podesta takes the stage at the Clinton viewing party and tells everyone to go home because things are too close to call. Electoral college votes so far: 218 Clinton, 248 Trump. On the television, Chuck Todd makes a huge sweeping motion over a map that is flanked in blue but hemorrhaging red and says, "She's gotta win *all* of 'em, as we said. He only needs one of them at this point."

like the highway is a conveyer belt delivering motorists to an immense
tequila sunrise. On clear mornings and early afternoons, it reflects the
bleached sky and appears as immaterial as a Mylar sheet stuck in the wind.

Yesterday I found myself at a red light less than a mile from the Strip.
A caved-in-looking homeless man gave another man—this one limping,
and seemingly detached from an accurate perception of his surroundings—shorts on his cigarette. There were no words exchanged; one man
just understood that the other needed a few drags and gave them to him. It
was the kind of gesture I might otherwise have stared beyond without reg-
istering, but the election had frayed everything inside me, leaving me raw
and in desperate need of encountering even the smallest instance of grace.

In adulthood—after being pushed out of the neighborhood where I
grew up by young professionals, becoming a permanent resident and then
a US citizen, and eventually landing a salaried job—I'd been able to sink
into the inertia of a relatively stable social life. I was learning to let myself
appreciate the unthinking assumption that when I opened my eyes in the
morning, there would still be a recognizable world there—a roof, electric-
ity, potable water, family. The day after the election, though, while living
in Albuquerque, a man with homemade tattoos snaking from his hands
to his throat came to turn on our floor furnace for the winter. He stared,
along with my wife and me, at the muted television screen in our living
room, on which Donald Trump stood before a row of American flags. The
furnace kicked on and burned a summer's worth of dead roaches, emitting
an acrid, loamy musk. The man told us how he'd grown up as a kind of
child soldier in an Albuquerque neighborhood called the War Zone, and
that his life had made a violent, steady descent, until somehow Christ had
intervened. He said it had happened when his friend was dissolved in a

bathtub. On the screen, Trump descended into a crowd, his face obscured by darkness, flashbulbs, and illuminated phone screens. The image cut wide and showed a constellation of red hats. The man shook my hand, shook my wife's hand, and then left. That he told us his story on that morning somehow made sense.

Since the election, that inertia had begun to slip into periodic bouts of vertigo, a roving sense of panic, general malaise, and moments of acute spiritual dislocation. I began to feel as though I wasn't living my days so much as wading through them. The real horror rooted itself in me after the initial bewilderment was washed away by the realization that this was not a radical departure from our past, but a logical end to the track we'd laid. Trump was not the cancer in our bones, but the dull pain we don't recognize until it's too late.

On November 9, at 1:33 a.m. eastern time, *USA Today* runs a story that begins, "There's a dimly lit cafeteria underneath Hillary Clinton's watch party in New York City and it may be one of the saddest places in the country right now." But when I see the photograph halfway down the page, it shows what appears to be a group of bored techies scrolling through Instagram. By mid-November, "friends" on Facebook are wishing for the return of the former civil-rights attorney who, as president, oversaw the forcible removal of more than three million undocumented immigrants. And by March 2, George W. Bush is jubilantly dancing onto Ellen DeGeneres's daytime talk show to Jean Knight's "Mr. Big Stuff," the host greeting him with a kiss on the cheek, just fifteen days before US-led coalition forces would slaughter, by their own count, "between 105 and 141 civilians"[A] in the al-Jadidah neighborhood in western Mosul. The nonprofit monitoring group Airwars deemed it "the greatest confirmed loss of life in any one civilian casualty event of the war,"[B] a war that the United States had officially withdrawn from in 2011 and rejoined in 2014, and that had cost, by some estimates, the lives of one million Iraqi mothers, fathers, sons, daughters, bakers, mechanics, bodybuilders, teachers, plumbers, clerics, doctors, welders, friends, and lovers.[C] As the soulful voice of Jean Knight—a singer born in New Orleans, a city that, like Mosul, Bush will forever be bound to by blood—croons over the universally recognizable bass line to "Mr. Big Stuff," Ellen attempts to wash away the rotten stench of war. They talk like old friends about portraiture, dog toys, family, and dancing. And while the studio audience applauds and laughs on cue, the absent subjects (Iraq, Abu Ghraib, and Maher Arar, the Canadian citizen disappeared by Americans at JFK airport and delivered to a year of torture in Syria[D]) roar in monstrous silence. Ellen tells Bush that "obviously the media was not, you know, great to you," as Mosul is reduced to eight million tons of rubble during urban fighting that is "described by US officials as the most intense since World War II," rubble that was combed for months for the bodies of missing loved ones, for which "there remains no official count of the dead."[E]

On September 5, Jeff Sessions appears on television wishing everyone a good morning. With the Department of Justice seal behind him, a light in his eyes, and his mouth twisted into a grin, he announces that an Obama-era executive action, the Deferred Action for Childhood Arrivals (DACA), is being rescinded. "No greater good [can be done] for the overall health and well-being of our republic than preserving and strengthening the impartial rule of law [sic]," he says joyously. He resembles Aldo Valletti in his role as "the President" in Pasolini's last and most rage-filled project, *Salò, or the 120 Days of Sodom*—a brutal film about the exertion of political power over those made subhuman. The President is among the most horrendous characters ever depicted on film, carrying out highly ritualized, violent, psychosexual games with a group of young captives. Perhaps the most disturbing aspect of his character is that his brutality is enacted with alacrity, and while observing most rules of decorum. "We are a people of compassion and we are a people of law," says Sessions as he carries out one of the only possible conclusions for DACA. "The compassionate thing is to end the lawlessness."

By September in the Las Vegas Valley, a visible layer of smog has been cooked into poison by the sun. The first summer under Trump is spent avoiding the outdoors, listening to the upstairs neighbor, a man in his fifties, scream obscenities at his elderly mother, and watching him tumble down the building's stairs at odd hours in blurs of rage and alcohol. After Sessions's announcement, I pace around my apartment, feeling ready to explode. I find myself grinding my teeth, peering out the window at the idiot across the parking lot whose wheels screech when he tears around corners in his white pickup with two giant American flags fixed on wooden posts. Before, I could mostly ignore it, but now all I can think about is that photo of a white man rushing at a black civil rights attorney with the sharp point of an American flag in Boston City Hall Plaza in 1976, and the photo of white rows of over thirty thousand KKK members, their faces exposed, waving American—not Nazi—flags as they march through DC with the American Capitol in the background.

An emergency community meeting is called in east Las Vegas. Around two hundred people pack into an auditorium. The mood is somewhat jovial, but there's a tension in people's bodies: whatever modicum of stability DACA recipients and their families had allowed themselves to feel is gone now. People are especially on edge because the government lured them into feeling secure, into providing their information, and now the possibility that it will be used to send people after them feels very real. After a few speakers, two brown-skinned people in their twenties, a man and a woman, step onto the stage. The young man raises the microphone and delivers a message about the Bar Removal of Individuals who Dream and Grow our Economy Act, or the BRIDGE Act, one of several bills proposed to Congress and the only one that doesn't include a pathway to citizenship. It's clear the two brown-skinned staffers have been sent to face the crowd by Republican senator Dean Heller, and almost immediately the crowd begins booing. Heller not only voted against the Development, Relief, and Education for Alien Minors (DREAM) Act in 2010, but also cosponsored a bill that would deny US citizenship to some children born in the United States. "I don't support amnesty," Heller said. "I don't support benefits for illegals. I don't support the DREAM Act. I don't support anchor babies."[F] The young man with the microphone rolls his eyes at the booing crowd and mumbles something about bipartisanship before he and the woman leave the stage. Someone near the back yells, "DREAM Act!," and then someone else shouts, "DREAM Act now!," and before they're off the stage, hundreds of people are chanting and shouting, drawing a line they feel prepared to hold.

A few moments of calm. I look around at the people who've come out for this. An older white man sitting up ahead wears a dark T-shirt with the white silhouette of a dove carrying an olive branch. It reads VETERANS FOR PEACE. A young woman with a child is furiously digging through a tote bag. She pulls her hand out like she's found what she's looking for—a piece of chewing gum. A teen boy with hair in his eyes sweeps it away and then places his hand back into the hand of the girl sitting beside him. An older Latina woman with fresh-looking highlights grips her purse and sits leaning toward the stage. A woman's voice comes over the microphone and everyone is asked to lower their phones, stop taking photos, and stop recording. There are a few large cameras on tripods in the room, probably from the news. The camera people look around at one another, pull off their headphones, and tilt the cameras down toward the floor. The woman then asks all the DACA recipients to stand. People shift uncomfortably in their chairs; many look around the room scanning for phones that might still be up and recording. From where I'm sitting, I see the three-quarter profile of a skinny teenage girl, maybe fourteen or fifteen, who is sitting in the row directly in front of me. She's surrounded by her teenage friends on both sides, girls with ripped jeans and new sneakers, bomber jackets and hoop earrings. She leans forward in her chair and then stands. She smiles and covers her braces with her right hand. Two hundred people applaud her and the other DACA recipients, who are all now standing. The moment collapses the brutality of the world as it exists and the horizon upon which our hope lives. A knot the size of a clenched fist turns in my chest as the applause roars and then eventually stops.

II.

We're told to park at the Erotic Heritage Museum, a building that looks like it houses an indoor swap meet. The exterior walls are the color of pale flesh. My wife goes into the lobby to ask if it is, in fact, okay for us to park there. When she returns, she's disappointed because a concept like "the erotic," she says, deserves so much more than looping videos, dildos in glass cases, and cardboard cutouts. "It deserves some real artifacts—at least as much marble as that piece of shit," she says, nodding toward our destination, the Trump International Hotel, that giant golden phallus in the sky. She says we should do like the Romans did to the Temple of Antoninus and Faustina at the Roman Forum, referring to *spolia*, the practice of scavenging and cannibalizing stone from already-existing relics. I remind her, though, that that particular attempt was unsuccessful, as we'd seen the grooves in the still-standing columns where marauders had attempted to bring them down. She shoots back: "You think any Vegas contractor hired by Trump can build something that'll last a thousand years?"

We walk toward the edge of the parking lot where several individuals wearing white T-shirts are talking to a few Metro cops in army green uniforms. They appear to be the organizers, and they're coordinating the march's route with the police, which doesn't surprise me, since the call for the march suggested wearing white and carrying American flags. This was something I'd seen before, but in this case it was particularly disturbing, given that Metro was one of the only metropolitan police departments in the United States to sign on to 287(g), an agreement with Immigration and Customs Enforcement (ICE) that essentially deputizes some local police as immigration agents in order to persecute and deport more people. Without prior knowledge of a protest, one can usually gauge what kind it is to a fairly accurate degree within the first few minutes of wading into the crowd. For example, if permanent markers are passed around at initial gathering points to write the National Lawyers Guild telephone number on some part of your body, or if someone is going around taking information for jail support, or if people are carrying bottles of white liquid, it means you haven't coordinated with the police and you might be involved in impeding the flow of traffic, occupying a building, trespassing, or entering into direct conflict with the police. I remember participating in a campaign in 2013, organized by a teenage girl named Tania Reyna, a Salvadoran priest named José Sigfredo Landaverde, and his congregation of poor and working-class immigrant families from Chicago's Little Village neighborhood. I was visiting my parents in Chicago and I'd heard they needed people. According to the activists with the congregation, area hospitals were excluding people without social security numbers from organ transplant lists unless they proved they had bank balances with enough money to cover several years of anti-rejection medication, which usually costs around fifteen thousand dollars a year.

A group of about forty of us marched from Landaverde's small storefront church on Twenty-Sixth Street to Northwestern Memorial Hospital— about seven miles away. Some of the marchers were elderly, others were several days into a hunger strike, many were extremely sick and in immediate need of organ transplants, most of us were poor and working-class. People took turns carrying black life-size coffins made of cardboard and signs demanding justice. One woman carried a framed photograph of her daughter, Sarai Rodriguez, who'd been denied a liver transplant by Northwestern and other area hospitals. Sarai had died two days before the march. Blanca Gomez, one of the protesters in need of a transplant, told a reporter about Sarai's death, and said that putting immigration status and money over people's lives was unjust. "That's not fair that they put paper over our lives."

It rained intermittently as we marched, making the black asphalt streets look alive, like the slick wet skin of an amphibian. When we arrived at the medical complex, the priest, Landaverde, requested a meeting with the head of the hospital to deliver the group's demands. When that meeting didn't happen, we marched up and down the downtown streets surrounding the hospital all day and well into the evening as medical professionals passed us on their way to lunch, and then again, hours later, on their way home. Our presence confronted them with the reality of being healers in a system that privileged capital over life. Most averted their eyes and pushed past us, but we were impossible not to see. A few news crews and photographers came to shoot footage and take photos. We passed out leaflets about our campaign, and when nighttime came we slept on the sidewalk across from the hospital. That night was the first time I'd slept outdoors in the city in which I'd grown up. Leaving a path in the middle, we slept on both edges of the sidewalk, and I fell asleep looking at the moonlit face of an older Mexican woman who'd lost all her fear.

When no one met with us the following morning, Landaverde smoked a cigarette, led a prayer, and talked with the congregation. The group decided we'd waited long enough. The priest asked us who had papers. Only a few of us raised our hands. He pointed to the coffins and said we would each pick one up, walk in a straight line across the street into the hospital, place our coffin on the floor of the lobby, and sit down until someone came to meet with us. I felt an unexpected but powerful aversion as we pushed past the hospital doors and entered the bustling lobby with tremendously high ceilings. I remember sensing that it was possible to cut through that feeling only because there were two people in front of me and two behind me. After a tense confrontation with several large security guards, someone from hospital management came down to speak to us, and after a few minutes agreed to set up a meeting.[2]

I think about this experience as we walk toward Trump International—about Sarai's mother sleeping in the glow of a streetlight two days after her daughter's death, about Blanca's clarity and Landaverde's militancy. A crowd of one hundred to one hundred fifty people snakes around onto Sammy Davis Jr. Drive, a street named for the singer who was denied accommodation at hotels where he performed to sold-out rooms, and who later campaigned for Richard Nixon, in '72. A pigeon whose right foot is a tight red knot without toes hobbles past us toward the street. It hops off the curb and is almost run over by a military Humvee advertising Battlefield Vegas—Las Vegas's "ultimate shooting attraction," where one can shoot "two hundred rounds in 1.3 seconds."

We cross the street and wade into the crowd. The sun, which is directly overhead, pounds through my shirt and makes my skin throb. Almost everyone wears white, and many people are wrapped in American flags or waving them at passing cars. I understand that not every protest has to be, nor should be, a form of direct action, but then what *is* the purpose of a protest like this? Behind us, a line of police stands in the shaded area of a concrete parking structure. They all stare blankly at the crowd. A few cars honk as they go by. The back window of a cab stopped at a red light goes down and a middle-aged white woman wearing a pink visor

---

2. A little over a year after this march, as well as other marches, campaigns, hunger strikes, and occupations, Illinois passed a law that would allow undocumented residents to obtain state-funded kidney transplants and money toward the anti-rejection medication necessary to make the transplants successful.

and sipping from a disposable cup squints behind her rhinestone glasses. She examines a protester's sign, one of the more colorful ones, which depicts Donald Trump as a pile of feces topped with his recognizable sugar-spun hair. It reads, RACIST NATIONALISM IS CACA, WE DESERVE MORE THAN DACA! She gives the crowd a thumbs-up and emits a cackle that quickly turns into a deep, wet cough as the cab screeches off.

The crowd is continuing to swell. Our line extends down the long block almost to the highway underpass. Standing next to me is a little girl who can't be older than four, wrapped in an American flag bigger than she is. I wonder what she understands about today, about the context in which we find ourselves, and who wrapped her in the flag. I presume the organizers called for white clothes and flags because of the images this would produce in the media, and how images like these would appeal to a broad swath of viewers. I imagine that a lot of the people who showed up are looking for catharsis, to satisfy the feeling that they're doing something against a regime that's intensified its attack. I know that's part of why I'm here, but is this enough?

A swarm of news cameras follows a man in a white button-down shirt tucked into pressed blue jeans as he crosses the street. As they approach I see that it's Ruben Kihuen, a tall, photogenic local politician who was elected to the House of Representatives in 2016. Kihuen described himself as the first DREAMer[3] in Congress but isn't actually, because he regularized his immigration status long before the 2001 introduction of the DREAM Act. Had he not been able to regularize at that point, he

---

3. Immigrants who would qualify for the various versions of the DREAM Act, or for DACA.

would have qualified for certain versions of the DREAM Act but would not have qualified for DACA, because he would have been one year and fifty-one days too old. I remember noting this discrepancy when reading about him in an article, and found it telling that rather than emphasizing how arbitrary and unjust these qualifications are, he simply chose to call himself a DREAMer.

When Kihuen and the television cameras arrive, the crowd reacts as though the homecoming king had appeared. People clap and wave their American flags for the TV cameras. People snap pictures with their phones while Kihuen smiles and leans in to pose for a few selfies. Kihuen and I share a similar trajectory in terms of when and how we immigrated and how we were able to regularize our immigration status. It's likely our families left Mexico for similar reasons—to cope with the economic misery that was in large part the result of predatory and indiscriminate lending by US commercial banks, the reverberations of the Volcker Shock throughout Latin America, the austerity plan imposed by the International Monetary Fund, and the economic liberalization schemes that followed.

Kihuen is a long-in-the-making star of the Democratic Party machine here in Nevada. He's been backed by Harry Reid, the formidable Culinary Union, and Nevada's sizable Latino voter base. A generous reading of his political career might be that he occupied space in a battleground state that could have been filled by someone much worse, and a less generous one might be that he helped manage some of the more politically active and unruly segments of Nevada's Latino voters for the

Democratic Party establishment. In the lead-up to the 2016 caucuses in Nevada, Kihuen, a superdelegate, fell in line with Clinton rather than backing Sanders, a candidate running on a platform that, almost point by point, would have disproportionately benefitted Latinos. The lesson of the Obama years, during which Kihuen worked for the Democratic machine in Nevada, was unambiguous: establishment Democrats, even former civil rights attorneys, will deport us in record-breaking numbers.[4]

This is a lesson Kihuen not only ignores but actively obscures for his "community" at every opportunity.

A voice booms over a bullhorn and the mass begins moving. Camera people and photographers run ahead to get footage of protesters holding signs that read: EDUCATION, NOT DEPORTATION, and OUR DREAM IS YOUR DREAM—THE AMERICAN DREAM. A cameraman shoots Ruben Kihuen and a couple of other politicians talking to people in the crowd.

---

4. What, exactly, this means has been disputed. Some commentators have argued that a change in definition of *deportation* inflated the Obama-era deportation numbers to their record-breaking status, implying that the change was only categorical. But the change that took place had very real, and very brutal, material consequences. In the past, people who were caught near the border, after having crossed it, were repatriated without going through the formalized deportation process. During the Obama era, migrants apprehended under similar circumstances were made to go through the formalized deportation process, meaning they were "counted" when they previously hadn't been, but also meaning they had a formal removal on their records. When someone with a previous removal is caught attempting to cross again, they are charged with a felony. According to the Pew Research Center, in 1992, immigration offenses made up 5 percent of cases in the federal courts; in 2012 this number rose to 30 percent. These inflated numbers also affect migrant communities by giving the impression that migration is on the uptick, which, in turn, facilitates the use of alarmist rhetoric for increased militarization and funding for repressive immigration enforcement.

We're on the opposite side of the street from the golden tower. Metal barricades run along the edge of the sidewalk and a line of Metro police in uniforms the same green as Border Patrol stand in the middle of the street. Groups of tourists enter and exit the large revolving doors of the hotel. Most of them glance at us momentarily, make no outward signs of acknowledgement, and hurry into or out of the lobby. To my surprise, one older white woman exits, squints in our direction, and gives us a thumbs-up. Less surprisingly, a stretch SUV limo pulls into the valet loading zone and about ten frat boys wearing layered polos with popped collars load thirty-packs of cheap beer into the vehicle. One of them lowers his head and stares over the brim of his aviators with a blank expression, then he laughs.

After a few minutes like this, we begin to move again. We pass an empty lot directly next to the hotel, where another Trump tower was supposed to stand. The president of the United States featured the plans for his two golden towers on his reality television show, but the second one never materialized: "Trump celebrated the opening of the first, and ultimately only, tower in April 2008, just weeks after the collapse of investment bank Bear Stearns, a prelude to the Wall Street meltdown."[G] Instead, there's an expanse of desert scrub that's cracked through the concrete, shards of broken glass, and trash surrounded by a crooked chain-link fence. At certain angles, the eastern facade of the golden tower reflects the image of the wasteland below it.

We round a corner onto the north end of the Strip, passing a loading dock, a service entrance, and huge dumpsters that emit the same sweet, rotten stench as an alley behind any restaurant. Hours ago, semis reversed onto these docks and workers rolled dollies of boxed foodstuffs into the building for their morning deliveries. Strings of uniformed workers filed into the service entrance at the back of the house, where all manner of invisible labor is performed twenty-four hours a day, seven days a week, three hundred and sixty-five days a year. The Strip occupies a mythic space in the American narrative, but in the light of day it's hard to see anything that isn't utterly common: exploitation, fast food, misery, substance abuse, sex work, obesity, joy, trash, and boredom. People may lose a great deal of money on an almost continuous basis in these casinos, but orders of magnitude more lose everything to hospital bills and mortgage lenders. At least here the casinos clearly post the odds.

One corner of a cut-up debit card lies in front of a place called Sugar Factory. Overhead, on a giant screen that usually loops ads the height and width of a two-car garage, there's a Windows error message that reads: A PROBLEM CAUSED THE PROGRAM TO STOP WORKING CORRECTLY. PLEASE CLOSE THE PROGRAM. Seven loudspeakers emit seven different pop songs, all of them bad, converging into a miasma that's recognizably English language but fails to carry meaning. It seems like every few hundred yards there are small plaques that list one or another of the Nevada Revised Statutes, things like PRIVATE ROAD AND SIDEWALK. NO TRESPASSING NRS 207.200, or RESORT DISTRICT: NO OBSTRUCTIVE USES PERMITTED ON PUBLIC SIDEWALKS AT LOCATIONS DESIGNATED BY WHITE STRIPES OR SIGNS PURSUANT TO CLARK COUNTY CODE CHAPTER 16.11. It strikes me as particularly ironic that there should be so many posted regulations in a place that advertises itself as a paradise of lawlessness and sin. To me, it looks like a Bruegel, if Bruegel had lived among vape shops, shopping malls, and food courts.

We chant and march as sightseers are momentarily confronted with a reality they are trying to escape. At some point, the sidewalk turns into a plastic dock under our feet. Two pirate ships, one white, one brown, float in a chlorinated pool littered with mini bottles of liquor and cigarette butts. A pair of sunburned tourists in neon tank tops, shorts, and flip-flops becomes trapped behind a wall of protesters as they attempt to get to the entrance of Señor Frog's. They're incredibly drunk and attempting to stand perfectly still, averting their eyes, as though we might not see them if they don't move. They gently sway in place. After we pass, a spark will crackle across their nerve endings and they'll resume their forward lurch toward barstools painted to look like white women's asses in G-strings. They'll order drinks, maybe frozen margaritas in plastic yardies that read SIZE DOES MATTER, or shots of tequila in neon test tubes. They'll pitch their heads back and see the ceiling, painted to look like the water's surface littered with three-dimensional inner tubes that surround women's asses. The asses bear the names of Mexican cities and towns they'll never pronounce correctly, where Americans nearly identical to them are, at the exact same moment, doing the exact same thing.

The heat begins to feel sickening. The sun is so bright it occupies the entire sky and doesn't look like an orb but like a blinding emptiness. I feel almost no relief when I recoil into the shade. We've reached the Mirage. I look to my right and see Aaron D. Ford, a state senator, and Ruben Kihuen, who somehow hasn't broken a sweat, being photographed carrying the march's largest banner. This is one of the photographs that will come to represent this march in the media. I lean against a fence for a moment, and almost immediately a stranger thrusts a cold, sealed bottle of water into my hands and makes a *drink it* gesture. I do.

Halfway through the bottle I see what I've been staring at—the Venetian across the street. Specifically, a replica of the Rialto Bridge that stretches over a street with no name that leads to the resort's entrance. On a trip to Venice, I'd visited a place called the Palazzo dei Camerlenghi, a white palace near the real bridge that housed, among other things, a debtors' prison on the first floor. Looking now at the replica, it seems like the casino floor is almost precisely where the debtors' prison is in Venice. A few hundred yards to the left, a winged lion, almost certainly made of plaster, ceramic, or plastic—not bronze like the real one—sits atop a column. It's one of the most recognizable symbols of Venice, a place that developed one of the first forms of governance to take shape under a nascent capitalism, where trade, commerce, military intervention, and state power produced one another. By the fourteenth century, it had become one of the wealthiest cities in Europe, and while much of the rest of the continent was still living under emperors or monarchs, in Venice the figure of the "sedentary merchant"[5] rose to power. Before this, merchants had sought ideal conditions for their commerce through movement, but the sedentary merchants of Venice found it advantageous to create their ideal conditions by shaping their immediate surroundings. They consolidated a government in which only members of their class could hold office; invented managerial techniques and financial instruments that allowed them to accumulate vast wealth;

---

5. A figure written about in *Business and Capitalism: An Introduction to Business History* by N.S.B. Gras, a professor at Harvard Business School who is credited with inventing the field of business history. According to Gras, the "sedentary merchant" (who established a home base for conducting commerce) marks a key transformation in the economic relations that led to modern capitalism.

instituted a police force that, at its height, numbered "one patroller to every 250 inhabitants"[H]; and developed a system of legal codes that could appear to be neutral, objective, and rational, rather than the arbitrary will of those in power.

On Las Vegas Boulevard, the Venetian is, like most other things here, real in its own way. The replica Lion of Venice casts a shadow on the sidewalk abutting the boulevard, a sidewalk the Venetian owns. When they were building the resort, the developers presented the county with a study they'd commissioned that recommended the widening of Las Vegas Boulevard to optimize traffic flow. This, however, would have required demolishing the public sidewalk, and, because of where the Venetian's property line lies, would have eaten up all available public space, leaving none for a public thoroughfare. After some back-and-forth, the state's Department of Transportation entered into an agreement with the Venetian allowing for the widening of the boulevard, so long as the resort owners built a sidewalk on their property. Less than a year later, when workers attempted to demonstrate on the sidewalk of the non-union casino, the Venetian began a sustained legal effort to ban these protected activities on spaces that have historically served as public forums.

Our mass of people winds up and over the pedestrian bridges that punctuate the boulevard. These are some of the only uncontested public spaces on the Strip, so buskers and homeless people tend to set up shop there. A man is keeled over in his wheelchair with a pint bottle of Malibu in his lap; another is splayed out and motionless, facedown on the ground. The sun is beginning to set and the facades of buildings polluted with neon advertisements project their glow onto the streets. A lone tourist up ahead says something to one of our group about breaking the law.

The man's face is angry, but he doesn't stop, because there are hundreds of us. This notion of "the rule of law" feels like one of the deeper, more pestilent ideological strains in the American mind. Not only is it reflexively used to legitimize brutality against immigrants, but it carries the implication that the law is sacred, neutral, and evenly applied, and that it exists independent of economic and political realities. None of this is true, but it works upon the world anyway.

After passing a fifth-sized version of the Brooklyn Bridge that runs over a fountain with a few inches of water in it, we arrive at our end point—the 150-foot Statue of Liberty on the corner of Las Vegas and Tropicana. A skyline like a low-resolution image of New York—missing pixels, collapsed distances, degenerated shapes—creeps over the statue's shoulders. Instead of twenty-seven thousand tons of copper and iron, she's made of a red iron frame wrapped in exterior drywall and Styrofoam coated in fiberglass. It's becoming night. Shadows swallow the stains up and down the boulevard, the stucco and drywall facades look almost like stone, and the drama of all the lights helps tell a story that isn't exactly true. Ruben Kihuen takes control of the bullhorn and delivers a version of one of his standard speeches, which is mostly him reminding us of all his personal accomplishments. "I'm here to tell you that if Ruben Kihuen can make it, all of you can make it!"[6]

The intended symbolism of ending the march here is obvious, but the mint green color of the statue is too even to look like the patina on the real thing. The eye wanders not to the replica of the Ellis Island

---

6. In mid-December, after he is accused of sexual harassment, Kihuen will announce that he will not seek reelection.

immigration building just behind the statue, but over it, to the red roller-coaster track just behind Lady Liberty's head. A few police in green uniforms are perched nearby, looking on, laughing at the whole scene. Almost a year from now, members of their department will arrest and hold an undocumented father under 287(g). His fourteen-year-old son, Silas, will visit him in jail, and on his way home will "quietly unbuckle his seat belt as his mom zoom[s] down the highway, open the driver's side back door and throw himself into oncoming traffic."[1] His father won't be allowed to attend Silas's funeral while he's held, awaiting deportation.

According to the Human Freedom Index, the United States is among the freest countries in the world.[7] The index makes this claim despite the fact that the US also has the highest number of prisoners worldwide, just under "2.3 million people in 1,719 state prisons, 102 federal prisons, 1,852 juvenile correctional facilities, 3,163 local jails, and 80 Indian Country jails as well as in military prisons, immigration detention facilities, civil commitment centers, state psychiatric hospitals, and prisons in the US territories."[J] The state of incarceration—perhaps the most literal and complete form of *un*freedom—in the US is so extreme that countries that "rank alongside the *least* punitive US states, such as Turkmenistan, Thailand, Rwanda, and Russia, have authoritarian governments or have recently experienced large-scale internal armed conflicts."[K] A report published by the Prison Policy Initiative found that "incarcerated people in all gender, race, and ethnicity groups earned substantially [41 percent]

---

7. The 2017 index ranked the US seventeenth out of one hundred fifty-nine countries. The index was copublished by the libertarian Cato Institute, the Fraser Institute, and the Liberales Institut at the Friedrich Naumann Foundation for Freedom.

less prior to their incarceration than their non-incarcerated counterparts of similar ages."[L] The Cato Institute, one of the libertarian institutions that collaborated on the Human Freedom Index, also released a report titled "Freedom in the 50 States 2017–2018," a ranking of "states by the policies that shape personal and economic freedom." In it, Nevada was ranked the fifth freest state in the country, despite having an incarceration rate that exceeds the United States', and that far exceeds that of any other Western democracy. Nevada's incarceration rate, for example, is approximately 5.5 times that of the United Kingdom, and 20 times that of Iceland.

State Senate majority leader Aaron D. Ford takes the microphone: "I am here with you because I am one of you. I'm not a DREAMer, but I dream like you." The crowd cheers. Their excitement rises over the chatter of the Strip to meld with the sound of several lanes of passing traffic. I look across the elevated walkways to the other side of the boulevard, wondering if anyone can hear us over the noise. Towering orange letters that spell H-O-O-T-E-R-S glow in the distance like a wildfire rushing toward us. A few people on the other side pause momentarily to look at us, then continue toward whatever their destinies might be on this particular night on the Strip. In the moment, cast in the soft darkness of early evening, Ford's affirmation is almost stirring, but six months before these words are spoken into the dusk, he "scuttled a hearing"[M] for a bill that, in its original version, sought to prohibit local police from carrying out immigration enforcement. The bill, SB223—even in its later, watered-down version, a version that narrowed its prohibition only to the police's point of contact with individuals, allowing local police to continue selling people to ICE for federal funds—was killed by opposition from police lobbyists, their collaborators in the state's Republican ranks, and by Democrats like Ford who found it "unwise"[N] to fight the Trump administration with us. Ford finishes his remarks with a few sentences in Spanish, and the crowd erupts as he passes the bullhorn.

A few days before the march, I read that when the United States Postal Service designed a forever stamp that featured the face of Lady Liberty, it unknowingly selected a photograph of the replica. What I'm looking at now is the statue at almost exactly the angle it appears on the stamp. I turn away to see a young woman in the crowd wearing butterfly wings that read UNDOCUQUEER. Right next to me, a father holds a small girl, maybe four or five years old, on his shoulders. Her voice cuts through the deep bass of the crowd: "The people united will never be defeated!" What can liberty mean, I think, when children younger than the girl I'm looking at now are locked in cages by successive American presidents from both parties? What does liberty mean when the pieces that are supposed to protect it are used to erect the architecture of racial and economic banishment, allow for the authoritarianism of the firm that employs you at will, the shop floor that you can't leave to go urinate, the drone, and the wall? Was it what sixteen-year-old Frederick Trump was after when he left the Palatinate and sailed across the Atlantic, passing, as he arrived, the copper pieces of the statue that were still in crates? Maybe no one knows what it is, because we've never seen it, or maybe it's among us, but we can't recognize it.

III.

I get off the train at Capitol South and sit down on a concrete bench to tie my shoe. The rush of the train departing, the chatter and bustle of people pushing past one another, and the escalator at the end of the station emit sounds like an Archie Shepp record. The coffered ceiling is reminiscent of the Pantheon and curves all the way to the tracks, making this space feel like a vault or mausoleum. It's cold in March on Capitol Hill. All I have with me is what I'm wearing, one change of clothes, and a notebook. It's the fourth, and tomorrow is Jeff Sessions's deadline for Congress to pass legislation to protect those who have DACA status.[8] The last few months have been tense, with immigrant groups all around the country ramping up their actions. There have been hunger strikes, campus campaigns, occupations of federal buildings, blockades at ICE facilities, and many other actions that have coalesced around the goal of holding the line at a "clean DREAM Act,"[9] which feels like a victory in and of itself.

The lettered streets in the Capitol area are sparsely peopled. I see only three individuals on my walk: a young white woman pushing a stroller, a white man with a briefcase rushing somewhere, and a Mexican worker retrieving something from his truck. The area is a strange confluence of quaint residential streets bumping up against monolithic government

---

8. The deadline is meaningless in two ways: thousands of immigrants have already lost the protections offered by DACA, and many more will be able to renew after March 5, 2018.
9. A "clean DREAM Act" is a DREAM Act with no money allocated to any border-security measures or immigration enforcement of any kind.

buildings that stretch for entire blocks. The gutters and sidewalks are impeccably clean, and I imagine the price of a home is well beyond the reach of anyone in the middle class. I remember reading somewhere that DC, the first black-majority city, lost its black majority during Obama's presidency. Something about the look of this place reminds me of Las Vegas, even though it appears so completely opposite. The columns, angles, and imposing blank walls evoke grandeur *and* austerity, power *and* restraint; the buildings suggest a lineage that hearkens back to the birthplace of republicanism and allude to a relationship between the people and power that isn't exactly true.

That night I sleep in a room with three other young men who've come to DC from Nevada. One is an organizer, one is turning twenty-one this evening, and another is a senior in high school who texts his girlfriend late into the night. She's somewhere nearby, in a room with the other women from our group, one of whom has been tasked with keeping an eye on her, at her parents' request.

March 5. Behind us, the Washington Monument fractures the pale sky, and up ahead the Capitol looks like a pile of bones. Looking over the heads of the people immediately surrounding me, I estimate that there are five hundred of us on the National Mall. This is both heartening and sobering. To put that number into perspective, around nine thousand people attended each lesser-attended game of the 2017 Texas high school football state championships. There were about forty-three thousand at the most attended game. Several hundred people wear orange-and-black-speckled monarch wings they'd painted the night before, making the lawns look like a wintering forest in Michoacán. A small cluster of PRESCHOOLERS FOR DACA, as it says on one of their caretakers' signs, play among themselves in sloganed T-shirts that go down past their knees. A yellow Lab wearing an orange CLEAN DREAM ACT T-shirt sits calmly in the crowd, sniffing at passersby and amiably receiving interested parties. A crowd of young people unfurls a giant rainbow flag the size of a shipping container.

There's an energy in the air that's hard to place. I, like many other people, came to the Mall today with only a photo ID and a fifty-dollar bill in my pocket. A good number of the activists and organizers here are undocumented, which makes their participation incredibly high-stakes. Talking to people here and elsewhere, though, I've gotten the sense that many feel compelled to seize the reins of this inchoate movement because its direction is up for grabs. In September, for example, a group of young, unruly immigration activists who refused to call themselves DREAMers took control of a Nancy Pelosi press conference in San Francisco. She'd selected a group of DREAMers to talk about their "experiences" in a way that would fit comfortably with the Democratic party line. Pelosi and Senate Minority Leader Chuck Schumer had begun negotiating with Trump on a bill that would trade the lives of some immigrants for others. Pelosi had assured the public she would support only a "clean" DREAM Act but also said she and Schumer were open to what she referred to as "technology or something like that." That "technology" amounts to swollen budgets for agencies dedicated to hunting and expelling immigrants and to what many defense contractors call a "virtual wall," made up of ground sensors, infrared cameras, surveillance towers, drones, helicopters, and blimps purveyed by defense contractors like Elbit Systems, the company that equips the apartheid walls around Gaza and the West Bank.

Short clips from the protest at Pelosi's press conference made the news, but all the televised segments ignored the most substantive parts of the activists' message, and mischaracterized what had actually taken place. CNN's Alisyn Camerota, for example, couldn't understand why the activists had targeted "Nancy Pelosi, who by all accounts is trying to protect the 800,000 DREAMers." Camerota had Democratic senator Jeanne Shaheen on the segment to theorize a reason for this kind of disruption. "Who knows who's stirring up this kind of animosity. What we know about the Russians and their interference in the 2016 elections is that they tried to increase divisions within this country. We saw it again in Charlottesville. So we don't know what is behind this." If they had just listened to what the activists had literally screamed at Pelosi, they would have heard what, exactly, was behind their interruption. Their message was multipart: (1) the United States bears huge responsibility for creating migration because of its predatory economic and military interventions throughout Latin America and the so-called third world, which means that (2) the US government owes a tremendous debt to the immigrants already here and to those who may need to come in the foreseeable future, and that (3) this debt can partially be redressed through immigration policy, and that (4) the Democratic Party has always collaborated in the ruinous policies that create migration and then criminalize and persecute immigrants.

These parts of the message weren't televised.[10]

---

10. The activists' cynicism toward the Democratic establishment was proved absolutely warranted when Democrats were presented with the opportunity to leverage a government shutdown by refusing to pass a spending bill that didn't include "clean" DREAM Act provisions. They refused to hold this line because of what it might have cost them politically moving forward, and they therefore bear responsibility for the horrors that followed.

The crowd begins to shift on the Mall. I'm among a mass of bodies, all moving in the same direction. Several lines form toward the center of the mass, and I take my place behind a wall of people walking with linked arms. There's a young man wearing a jacket and tie with an orange headband knotted around his forehead. He gazes far beyond the people in front of him, as if he were in a trance. Ivon, a middle-aged casino worker, also from Nevada, told me a deeply personal story about how and why she became an activist. Now she has young children at home, and says she was protesting when she was pregnant with her little girl, and that once her baby could leave the house, she was in the streets with her. People have come from Tennessee, Nevada, New York, Arkansas, Florida, Arizona, Colorado, Washington, Pennsylvania, and elsewhere. This is the fourth, fifth, and sixth time some of these people will march on the Capitol, and when they go home, some of them to deep red states, they'll help organize students, workers, and immigrants in local campaigns. Many of the people here today aren't old enough to drink at a bar.

The river of protesters veers off the lawns of the National Mall and onto Jefferson Drive. A middle-aged black man sitting in the driver's seat of a small passenger bus takes photos of us as we pass. He raises a clenched fist out his window. A white woman with two children leaving the Smithsonian Castle freezes as she exits. The children, about four or five years old, look up at her and then back at us. Some of us wave, and the two children wave back. In the spring of 1968, after Martin Luther King Jr. was assassinated, US marines mounted a machine gun on the steps of the Capitol, about one hundred yards from where we are now. As cited by the *Washington Post*, thirteen thousand soldiers, "the most to occupy an American city

since the Civil War," were set loose on people pushed beyond their limit.
A few years after that, soldiers protesting the American war in Vietnam
threw their Purple Hearts, Silver Stars, and other commendations "over a
wire fence that had been hastily erected in front of the Capitol and [they]
landed at the feet of the statue of Chief Justice John Marshall." Today is
not that. Despite the mass of us here today, the left operates from a place
of almost complete defeat—it can hardly be said that there is a left with
any real capacities, but I've been in rooms where people confront questions
that might begin to build toward something enduring: what should our
relationship to electoral politics be? How can we institutionalize leftist
organizations independent of the donor class? What are realistic but prin-
cipled goals we can set as a concrete political agenda?

We cut across C Street and come to the Rayburn House Office Building, an austere marble structure that nullifies a city block with over one
hundred US representatives' offices. It conjures the sterility of something
long dead, like a chalk desert or a bleached coral reef. Nothing about its
exterior feels like it was made for the living, and I imagine its interior
as a series of winding halls lined with thousands of rows of file cabinets
containing nothing but information about its own baroque filing system.
As we walk by, an old, bald white man in a gray suit, with white hair
and gray skin, stands at one of the large, rectangular windows cut into
the stone. He looks down at us and shakes his head conspicuously before
he recedes into the darkness of his office.

We arrive on the lawns on the east side of the Capitol. The column of
protesters curls around several dozen metal stakes that have been driven
into the grass. A few speakers tell their stories through a bullhorn that's
passed around, while others tie paper flowers to the stakes, which spell

U-N-A-F-R-A-I-D in colorful letters. I stare up at the white dome. Ivon appears from between a group of young people; she's wearing black leggings with Día de los Muertos skulls on them. She asks if I'm ready. I nod and tell her I'll be right behind her. The crowd shifts. A group of nineteen imams and other Muslim community leaders breaks away and heads toward the Capitol. A second column descends toward the intersection of Independence and New Jersey Avenues, just beside the Capitol. A multitude of voices over bullhorns works the crowd into a controlled frenzy: *"Undocumented! Unafraid! Undocumented! Unafraid! Undocumented! Unafraid!"*

About five hundred people occupy the intersection. The very center of the mass forms an inward-facing circle. A second concentric ring forms around them, and a third around the second. I'm part of the third ring, and I'm looking in at Ivon, a working-class mother, in the center. She and the others in the middle two rings drop to the ground, while we in the third ring push outward against the crowd. I can feel my heartbeat in my ears and in my fingertips. The people in the center begin quickly chaining themselves together around their midsections and ankles. The people in the second ring face inward and bind their hands together with segments of PVC tubing. Once the central rings are bound and in position, we in the third circle sit facing outward, back to back with people in the second ring. I am leaning against Bud, an old white man from Florida, who tells me he loves me. "I love you, too, Bud," I respond, and mean it. I hold hands with the two women next to me. One is a bartender from New York City with purple hair; the other was a participant in the second Freedom Summer. The organizers get everyone else onto the sidewalks that face our three circles.

About sixty Capitol Police arrive in cars, on bikes, and on foot, including a sergeant in a white shirt. The woman to my right, who was in Mississippi in 1964, squeezes my hand as I watch her scream at the police. The woman to my left sits quietly with her eyes closed. Through my back, I can feel Bud breathing and chanting. It's a while before the sergeant gets on a bullhorn and officially tells people to disperse. No one does. He issues a second warning, then a third. He instructs the other officers to make their way around the outer circle and to tell us we have one last opportunity to get up and leave before we're placed under arrest. The cops make their way toward us. Bud tells me he loves me again and I tell him I'll see him on the other side. The bartender from New York begins to shake as the officers tell her she has one last chance to go. I squeeze her hand twice and she squeezes mine back. They pick her up and take her away to a staging area they've cleared on the street. They bind her hands behind her back with plastic cuffs. An officer looks down at me and tells me the same thing. The woman to my left squeezes my hand, and I tell him I'm not leaving. They pick me up and take me away.

It takes hours for the cops to cut through the PVC and the chains and arrest all of us. Sixty-eight are arrested at the intersection of New Jersey and Independence. Forty of us are charged with "crowding, obstructing or incommoding." The people who chained and bound themselves are hit with an additional charge of resisting arrest. The group of nineteen who'd broken away earlier are arrested inside the Capitol while trying to get into Paul Ryan's office. As we're bussed to a booking facility, I sit with the strangers whom I haven't gotten to know, but in whom my hope now lives. We're seated in a large warehouse with long tables where police sit, ready to process us. They call us one by one, and as people's names are read aloud, we cheer. We cheer eighty-seven times over the course of five or six hours, and as each person is released, they exit the warehouse into a cold night, where a crowd of those who have just been freed huddle under a streetlight, waiting to cheer again.

ENDNOTES

A. Hopkins, Alex. "Airwars annual assessment 2017: civilians paid a high price for major Coalition gains." Airwars, 18 Jan. 2018

B. Ibid.

C. Goldenberg, Suzanne and Jonathan Steele. "What is the real death toll in Iraq?" *The Guardian*, 19 Mar. 2008

D. Mayer, Jane. "Outsourcing Torture." *The New Yorker*, 14 Feb. 2005

E. Oakford, Samuel. "Counting the Dead in Mosul." *The Atlantic*, 5 Apr. 2018

F. Snyder, Riley. "Indy Fact Check: Rosen says Heller opposes DREAM Act, but senator's moderate views leave no clear-cut answer." *The Nevada Independent*, 27 Sept. 2017

G. Mishak, Michael. "Trump's tower a sore spot on the Strip." *The Los Angeles Times*, 30 April 2011

H. Ruggiero, Guido. *Journal of Criminal Law and Criminology, Law and Punishment in Early Renaissance Venice*, vol. 69, issue 2, summer 1978

I. Bekker, Jessie. "Dad relives night son died on US 95 in tearful jailhouse interview." *Las Vegas Review-Journal*, 24 Aug. 2018

J. Sawyer, Wendy and Peter Wagner. "Mass Incarceration: The Whole Pie 2018." Prison Policy Initiative, 14 Mar. 2018

K. Sawyer, Wendy and Peter Wagner. "States of Incarceration: The Global Context 2018." Prison Policy Initiative, June 2018

L. Kopf, Daniel, and Bernadette Rabuy. "Prisons of Poverty: Uncovering the pre-incarceration incomes of the imprisoned." Prison Policy Initiative, 9 July 2015

M. Messerly, Megan. "Cancela: Amended immigration bill will not move forward now." *The Nevada Independent*, 28 Mar. 2017

N. Ibid.

I WANT A FRIEND

BY EMMA COPLEY EISENBERG

MAYBE IT WAS ONLY the mood I was in that night—bitter, biting, yet full of loose energy—that led me back to the queer bar, a place I'd sworn I'd never go again. By then I had no grand hopes left for love, but was propelled instead by quite another purpose: I wanted a friend. Not just any friend. I wanted *the* friend, the friend who is the stuff of movies and books and love songs—the friend who sees, the friend who gets, the friend to whom you have to explain nothing and who is yours until the end of time.

All afternoon and into the gloaming, I'd been sitting in the dark, watching my screen and polishing off a bottle of screw-top rosé, precisely the kind of blissful combination my other self disapproves of. What was the deal with Tony Soprano, finally and after all? So beautiful, so angry.

Then it was time to go. On the metro, two girls sat side by side in matching floral dresses and cursed each other over tiny hands made of butterfly wings. The exit tunnel and escalator smelled like important documents burning, which is the best description of Paris as a whole that I am capable of offering.

My potential new friend was a woman I'd met on Twitter when she'd liked a picture of my cat. Cute cat, she'd commented. What's his name?

I told her his name—yes, like the angel—and she launched into a monologue about the Holy Trinity, which is my actual favorite subject to debate. Three into one, one into three. It makes no sense, yet it makes sense. *I agree, utterly and totally*, this woman said. In her little photo, she wore a droopy yellow bow in her hair. Here, I remember thinking, was a person who did not play by the world's rules.

As usual, the filmmaker and her girlfriend stood in the street outside the bar smoking the cheapest possible kind of cigarettes. They greeted me with kisses in a tired kind of way, turning their faces to mine so that only the corners of our chins touched. Once upon a time, I had caused a lot of trouble here, both emotional and physical, so I understood their loyalty.

The signs asking for donations to fund the bar's legal fees had come down, and I wondered what this meant. The bar had opened in a disreputable neighborhood that over time had become reputable, triggering a campaign from its new neighbors to close it down for reasons of sound and sexuality. But this argument does not play out the same way in France as it would in America, I have learned, for though the French surely have their own confusions of object and symbol, they are generally unimpressed by binary thinking. It's an immunity I am still trying to acquire.

Over my large plastic cup of good beer, I watched the butch-femme couples kiss each other with their tender fish mouths and surveyed the gaggles of androgynes in vests made from various shades of denim who occupied the couches in the graffiti-soaked back room. I had the feeling again then, the only feeling that makes my other self shut up and listen.

Once, as a teenager in Virginia, after feeling the feeling for a whole year, I drove to a shooting range/gun store and looked at the big sign. GUNS, it said, ALL SHAPES AND SIZES. My friend's older brother worked inside, and I knew I could be successful if I wanted to be. Success, in this context, would be a lovely rectangular gun, very small and possibly silver, held to the right side of my head and fired. Did I want to? My other self was silent as I sat in the car and silent when I pulled the car back onto the two-lane, back onto I-95 and through all the miles home. The decision was mine.

According to the clock above the bathroom with pictures of cats for numbers, my potential new friend was late. I saw one girl I thought was cute, in a black denim button-up onesie—little tits, no bra—which was just the kind of garment I would like to wear but never would. By the time you got the pants on and fastened in just the right way, you'd have no energy left for the top.

Here is the thing: I had a friend once, for three years. One day it was all, Let's write our names on a cheap gold lock and lock it to this bridge. It was I who went to the hardware store and bought the lock, but she who wrote the initials in Sharpie and plopped the little key into the water. To be fair, the lock was so cheap that the U of it kept coming out altogether, so I helped my friend jam it back in once it was around the thin iron trestle. We also wrote vows, promising to bring more joy into each other's lives rather than less and to remind each other that we are both special and talented and destined for great things. This is a kind of marriage, I said, and it means we are together now, until the end of time. Okay, she said.

Maybe I should have better clarified the terms, or even then picked up on my friend's tone of hesitation. But there's a reason for that extra *F*—it's not "best friends for now, until we tire of each other." Object permanence, my other self was fond of telling me, is not your forte. She may have been right, that other self. Yet here is what she did not know: people leave. People quit. People pack up and move on.

Later, my ex–best friend forever stayed at my apartment for five days while deciding whether to begin an affair with a man who was not her husband. My cat purred between her breasts. It's been so long since I've felt free, she said. I've never told anyone these things before, she said. I know, I said. We ordered noodles delivered by an Italian man on a slick red scooter and it was she, not I, who made the smart and mocking comments about the likely size of his cock. We watched a movie about the Italian mafia, how it extends its tentacles into every corner of Italian life, even into the trash cans and the gardens. Do you ever feel, she said, that your body is like a garden full of trash, and that the longer you live, the more trash you dig up, until you think you are done digging up trash and then you dig up the biggest piece of all? Yes, I said.

All that night, as my ex–best friend and I lay turned away from each other in my big bed, my other self spoke to me in aphorisms. *Keep no secrets, tell no lies; love is a verb, not a noun; if you love someone, set them free.* I didn't know how exactly these related to my situation, but I listened to her words, took what I wanted, and left the rest. I understood that there were some things—marriage, for example—against which, if I fought, I would lose every time.

In the morning, my ex–best friend was no closer to a decision, so it was I who sent her packing back to her husband with half a loaf of the banana bread we'd made. Meow, the cat said when she left with her big, shiny backpack, which protected all her most important belongings from the elements. Her grid-lined notebooks and her Muji pens and her big jade necklace and her tarot cards and her rock that I had given her, which absorbed her sadness. Meow, the cat said again, when she called to say she had decided to stay with her husband and marry him again in her mind. There was static in the connection, my other self trying to speak. I ignored it. But what about how he tramples your spirit? I said. I never said that, she said. Hadn't she?

First came the series of small miscommunications, then the one bad lunch at the bakery, then finally the email: Never call me again. Don't text. Don't tweet. Don't like me, don't tell my story, etc. I know I am no picnic to love, that much has been made abundantly clear time and again, but this I thought I would never, as long as I lived, understand. What kind of person slams the door on love in so loud a manner, plus so quick, and forever? What kind of person puts all their vital blood into a single arm and then cuts off the arm? Whack, whack, whack.

There was no continuity, there was no longevity, there was no forgiveness, it seemed. The snake did not eat its tail but instead kept eating pieces of experience and shitting them out. I felt like that snake—renewed and empty, with no direction to go but forward. How many times had I moved, how many cities had I ploughed through, in the decade between childhood and real life? Paris was the fifth or the sixth, depending on your definition of residency.

While I sat waiting, I drank my big plastic beer and then I drank another and I listened to the music play. The clock had left its position at the orange cat and now pointed to a gray Maine coon cat with a luxurious white tail. I opened the glass door and stood in the street. The bouncer had taken off her suspenders and they fell onto her big thighs like strange and beautiful shackles. I asked the filmmaker if she had a cigarette. She gave me one and even offered to light it for me.

Where have you been? she asked, without too much meanness. We've worried.

Oh, here and there, I said. The university has been on strike so I've been listening to all the speeches.

Don't listen too hard, she said. Eventually, it's just the same guy, over and over again.

She smiled. *Viens avec nous*, she said, gesturing to her girlfriend and then down the street. We're going for falafel. She crushed her cigarette beneath her Converse shoe.

My ex–best friend forever called these Chuck Taylors because she is from the Midwest, though there could have been some other reason.

I can't, I said. I'm waiting for someone.

I watched them turn the corner and then I watched two baby dykes make out furiously against the dirty window of the laundry next door.

The streets were dark and friendly and the world was truly huge and glittering, I remember, despite the way it had been treating me.

She never showed, that new friend. Later, a message appeared saying that she had been caught in a terrible rainstorm (she was taking the metro in from *les banlieues*) and asked if we could reschedule—a rain check. Ha ha ha, my other self said, what a dumb joke. No, I wrote back.

I never did find another friend like the one I'd lost, and if I had known that then like I know it now, I would not have continued living. But it is possible, I have discovered, to supply that kind of friendship to oneself, if you work very hard at it, and practice every day. I'm doing it now, even as we have been talking all this time, even with you here.

DELANDRIA

BY ASALI SOLOMON

THE STREETS OF THE town could in no way be described as lively during the day, but at night they were even more deserted; the neat brick streets and ornate Victorians resembled the outcome of a pristine little purge. Rumor was that the students occasionally slipped into town after dark, calling at a certain ramshackle house to secure pills or powders too specialized to be found on campus. She almost never saw them.

Magna sped as she approached her apartment building, on Main Street, which was as desolate as it had been when she'd set out earlier that night. Suddenly a brown-and-white blur reared up in front of her. Meaning to hit the brake, she stamped on the accelerator. There was a violent, wet crunching sound and a scream caught in her throat.

With the helpless terror she'd felt at the top of roller coasters, she did not stop.

BEFORE

It had become a habit for Magna—watching television, drinking wine, and then going for a drive. She and Jamal had ritually drunk wine while watching television every night, despite the fact that back then everyone in academia could be heard saying, "Oh, I never watch TV." Since no one in academia ever said, "Oh, I never drink wine," she wondered if they perhaps preferred to sip staring into the abyss. But eventually Jamal swore off TV, saying he wasn't getting enough done on his dissertation. Then he gave up drinking. Then he left her.

That was when Magna added the drives. It felt healthy to go out into the sharp air after the solo slide into the musty depths of the couch. Tonight she had given herself a quick assessment and decided she was okay to drive. She worried a bit about the fact that she had begun crying unexpectedly at the episode in season one when Wallace gets killed. She had not cried the first time she'd seen it. But poor Wallace! He had tried so hard to take care of the neighborhood kids, even though he was just a kid himself. Magna sobbed, remembering when the actor had been a hopeful teenager readying for the prom on *All My Children*. Nevertheless, grabbing her keys off the nail by the door, she concluded that she was not drunk, just sad. It was a sad time, on this show and in her life.

The apartment building, a wide colonial, was quiet except for the blare of Mr. Oakley's TV set, which ran constantly, game shows during the day, weather and shopping channels at night. Mr. Oakley was a very nice, stooped old man, the type who looks like a baby, with an open smile. His loud TV and the large NRA bumper sticker on his car were the only problems with him as a neighbor. Magna never saw or heard anybody else in the building. She often wondered if she and Mr. Oakley were actually just roommates. The landlord was an upbeat, platinum-haired woman who lived elsewhere and suggested that Magna use "old-fashioned elbow grease" on the thick coatings of bird shit that had covered her back window and porch since before she'd moved in that summer.

Once outside, Magna inhaled the night. The stars looked crowded and close. "God's own country," she had always said to Jamal when they saw something pretty in this new town, which was often. She felt grateful to him for accompanying her to this hellhole, and was anxious to highlight its meager charms. And it was true that even the dump had a pastoral allure. "God's own country," she'd said among the soiled mattresses and splintered wood, where they'd come to bring a broken IKEA shelf that she shouldn't have packed in the first place. He'd laughed that time, holding his nose. After a couple of weeks she'd known it was becoming annoying, but she couldn't stop saying it.

"That's becoming a tic," he'd said.

"You say that about everything that gets on your nerves," she'd said.

"*Or* maybe you have a lot of tics."

Before he left, she and Jamal had sat on the second-floor back porch amid the bird shit and he had declared that the night sky was the only thing he would really miss. Oh, and her, of course; of course he'd miss her. Then he'd actually attempted a kiss. This was just after he'd announced that he was going back to California, where they'd been graduate students, because he felt like there was something special with Ananda, and he just had to figure everything out. He clarified that he wasn't breaking up with Magna at all, just putting things on pause. Instead of meeting his lips, Magna had put up an elbow, which he didn't see because his eyes were closed. She hurt his face and was not sorry.

Sometimes it was hard to remember why she had been with Jamal. Mostly he was the prototype of the bad boyfriend in a Tyler Perry movie. But then she would remember—he was handsome, smart, black, and well lotioned, the most undeniable man Magna had ever dated (like the bad boyfriend in a Tyler Perry movie). He had been several cuts above the other men in her graduate program. They were head cases: this one pretending to be gay to get closer to straight women; this one who'd written all of his coursework essays about feces; this one wearing an undershirt to class, approaching undergrads in Payne Hall, saying, "Can I holler at you for a minute?" Jamal, on the other hand, was beloved by everyone, and lived on secret fellowships that only the secretary and the department chair, and eventually Magna, knew about.

For the first few years in the program, he and Magna had been friends while he was on and off with a chalky black art history student who looked like a Goya painting. When that woman got a job in Texas off of one dissertation chapter and Magna found herself in bed with Jamal, she couldn't believe it. She got high off the look on people's faces when they walked into a room together.

Before him, she'd never wanted children, but even with how unhappy they had begun to make each other, even after he left, she still ached to one day parade the streets with his baby in a stroller. It was a fantasy so familiar that it had become memory, painful to recall.

*   *   *

As she drove down the dark street, past the quaint stores selling mugs and Lilly Pulitzer dresses, the Confederate junk shop and the one good restaurant, Magna knew she was trying escape from what had happened that afternoon, her meeting with the university president. He was trim, silver-haired, with burnished but not shiny shoes and the sharp facial planes of a film actor, but a Bill Clinton nose, a red medicine dropper there at the tip. She'd had to meet with him because she'd made the mistake of telling her most sympathetic colleague, the most liberal person in the English Department, about a slightly menacing incident, and the colleague had been upset enough to contact the president. "I hope it's okay," she'd said, only after she'd set up the meeting. Magna had said it was okay, feeling a sense of excited doom.

In the president's office Magna had found it hard to explain herself. She imagined that he'd postponed something more significant to take this meeting—a fund-raising call, a preliminary interview for an even fancier job, two fingers of whiskey. Was her story even a story? Two days earlier, she had been standing on the street near her apartment building when a car drove by and a male voice yelled, "Hey, girl!" in a voice like one of the Negro crows in *Dumbo*. She had heard laughter and saw a flash of white boy, clearly students at the school—they had a university bumper sticker. It was meant to be an imitation of her, Magna—how she would say "Hey, girl," because she was black.

"Hey, girl," she cawed to the thick burgundy carpet, the beautiful stone fireplace, and the portraits of landed gentry. She did not mention the crows in *Dumbo* to him, but the president nodded with some understanding. Magna had the absurd thought that she wished the boys in the car had instead called her a name, a historically certified epithet, which would have made for a better narrative. That had happened once back in her hometown, Philadelphia, a heavily black city that was also home to a lot of hateful white people. She'd been standing on a corner near her high school, headed to her therapist's office, and a girl's voice had screeched out of a passing car: "Nigger!"

"There is a need," the president said, after Magna's plotless yarn about the boys in the car, "for more dialogue about these issues." Here he paused as if someone were taking notes and needed to catch up. "I hope you always feel comfortable speaking about these things. And I hope that we can stay in touch." When his eyes drifted toward the door, she smoothed her skirt to stand.

As she saw herself out, Magna recalled the thin, quivering lip of her white colleague. She wasn't the only one who became distressed when Magna told her what it was like to be in the town and in the school; it was as if the well-meaning white people who'd been here for years, expatriates who had all gone just a tiny bit native, were meeting reality anew through her eyes.

"You can leave the door open," she heard the president say but she had already gently closed it.

There were other things Magna would have told him if he had wanted to know about her life here at Lashington & Wiis. About how she was regularly mistaken for a student and told (with some stiffness) that this mistake was a compliment. About correcting the word *colored* in student essays. About the roiling sea of Bush-Cheney stickers on shiny SUVs in the parking lot (though who knew where the political sympathies of the university president lay?).

She could have told the president about how Benton Anders, a freshman from South Carolina in her Narratives class, had responded to Magna's "fun" assignment, a three-page imitation of June Jordan's memoir, *Soldier: A Poet's Childhood*. Benton Anders had attempted to imitate the deliberately childlike tone of Jordan's prose to rhapsodize about a woman named Delandria, his nanny from "baby all the way to eighteen." (He was currently eighteen). Delandria was described by Anders as "cocoa brown" and "pillowy." He had apparently missed the venomous irony of Jordan's child-voice, which describes the violence, abuse, and insanity of her childhood; his piece culminated in a particularly cherished memory of riding a carousel at age sixteen while Delandria stood on the side, waving in the hot sunshine. "When I think of family, I think of my Deli," he had written. It didn't help matters any that Benton Anders called Magna "ma'am" instead of "professor," and that she had been too alarmed to correct him at the beginning and that then it had become too late.

"You must think it's cute," Jamal had said. Magna didn't think it was cute, not really, but Benton Anders was cute. That was undeniably true. He was over six feet tall with curly dark hair and light blue eyes. But he was less cute looming over her in her office in his pajamas, smelling beery and chemical, that time he'd overslept, missed class, and come running in five hours later to turn in his second paper. It said right there on the syllabus, "NO LATE PAPERS," and it seemed to Magna that, as a new black female professor barely out of her twenties, there were two ways to play this. She'd chosen the way in which they'd call her "professor" (even as her colleagues were "Lisa" and "Charley") and she'd point to the line that said "NO LATE PAPERS."

"So that's a zero?" he said. "But it's worth 5 percent of my grade!"

"There will be plenty of opportunities—"

There had been an exciting sequence of expressions and colors in the face of Benton Anders, as he had gone from slouching to erect and out of her office. He returned to her office fifteen minutes later, the flannel-shirted department chair in tow. With a hand on the shoulder of Benton Anders, Charley had backed Magna in a paternal I-wouldn't-do-it-like-this-they're-just-kids-but-I-get-it way, but she barely heard what he was saying for the shock: the child had run straight upstairs to the department chair to tattle on her. She tried to imagine herself, over a decade ago, a freshman back at the University of Pennsylvania, going to the department chair because of something a professor had done.

Even as the campus sat still and dark, she could feel it radiating malevolence toward her passing car. There in the grand Greek houses, the white students stayed up late to haze and rape each other; the black students crowded into dorms, testifying angrily and creating escapist personal dramas; the gay students hid under their beds, praying over transfer applications. Over it all, in the center of town, in front of the campus gates, there was the statue of General Lashington and his horse, Colonel Wiis, keeping faithful watch. Magna stifled the impulse to hold her breath while passing it.

As the town gave way to country, and the roads become more poorly lit, she could still see the rebel flags affixed to the houses. Her childhood was whatever the opposite of a rebel flag is; there was an invented Swahili grace, counterintuitive black supremacist narratives of world history, the spelling of *Afrika* with a *k*, and *Amerikkka* with three. But she'd had to take this job; she could no longer hide in graduate school. Her father had died of a heart attack that they had all seen coming but could not swerve to avoid, and her mother was comforting herself in an expensive apartment near the Philadelphia Museum of Art, hoping to die before her money ran out. Any day now, Magna's corporate attorney brother-in-law was going to be indicted on fraud charges, and Magna's sister would have to move back to the city with her two small children. The job Magna had been offered was in *this* place—not the place in Southern California whose English department had so many black professors that she'd gotten hairstyling ideas on the campus visit. They had given that job to someone with more interesting scholarship and better hair.

Magna arrived at the spot where you could really begin to see the mountain across a meadow. She had driven farther than she usually did at night; this was a spot she'd previously been to only during daylight hours. Shortly after Jamal had left, which was around the two-year anniversary of her father's death, she'd come here to look at the autumn leaves. It had not cheered her up, because even when no one died or left you, and even though she knew Jamal would eventually drop Ananda, too, fall was incontestably fucking sad.

She had picked up the phone three times tonight to call Jamal, to tell him about the university president. But it was not a reason to break their silence, just as the story she'd told the president was not quite a story, but an ugly little nothing.

Magna looked at the dark shapes of trees and the mountain looming ahead. She thought of the many horror movies she'd seen that included a version of this sequence, a clueless person alone in the woods. Not for the first time, she imagined running from slave catchers, and lamented that she had no notion of the direction of the North Star. After walking a few brisk paces in no particular direction, she decided to head back to what was home.

AFTER

Had she maimed a person? Had she killed him? Fear squeezed her chest as she drove away from the accident, in the opposite direction she'd driven earlier—away from the woods and toward the towns that were worse than this one. Her heart thudded erratically and she cursed rhythmically to try to calm herself. Along this road there were no antiques shops or heralded berry pie and peanut soup (the slaves invented that!). These towns had no tourist offices bearing pamphlets about the General, his noble fight for family and the land worked by God-given slaves. In this direction were fly-specked diners, a massive Goodwill complex, hand-lettered signs, and abandoned gas stations. But just as it is purportedly darkest before dawn, she mused that if she drove all night through the worst of towns, she might greet the sunrise in Washington, DC. Perhaps someone would hide her in a garret and help get her to New York. Maybe NYU had a job in her field this year? Soaked in sweat, she lowered the window, which brought on violent shivering. She rolled it back up.

In her mind she saw the prosecution reading off her privileges as the small-town Southern jury weighed her fate. (A subliminal flash of the yellow cover of *To Kill a Mockingbird*.)

"The defense will say that this woman was slowly driven crazy by so-called racism as if dying by one thousand cuts. But this woman was no slave! *Slavery ended over one hundred years ago!* And if attending good schools and being raised by a loving family and earning a PhD *unharassed* and a teaching position at one of the most elite schools in the country is slavery, then shackle me up, ladies and gentlemen, because slavery is the best deal in town!"

Magna felt herself swerving into the U-turn.

Back on Main Street, she parked the car with some deliberateness and walked over to the boy's long, twisted body, which he'd managed to drag out of the road and close to the curb. Though it was late November and near the mountains, he wore no jacket, just a pink, rumpled Oxford shirt and thin pants, no socks. "Help," he whispered. She knew that in his mind he was yelling; she knew because they were sharing a nightmare. He didn't seem to recognize her, though they saw each other twice weekly, every Tuesday and Thursday from 1:15 to 2:30 p.m., excepting his two absences (so far).

"There's been an accident," she said, clamping her cell phone to her damp cheek with her shoulder as she used her hands to drape her sweatshirt over him. "Someone was hit."

She had called the police only once before, and it had been in this town. Not 911, but the other number, the one you call in a more leisurely manner, about nuisances. She and Jamal had been in bed listening to something she had not heard before or since—a party at a house nearby. Earlier that evening, while they had been watching television, arguing about their future during the commercials, the party had been background noise. But eventually they had lain awake, their argument unresolved, and the party had continued insistently. The town's usual silence had felt aggressive; Magna had been surprised to find this was worse.

At 2:30 a.m. people yelled, "Whoooooooo!!!!!"

"I'm calling the police," she said.

"Don't," murmured Jamal. "That's bullshit. You're gonna call Boss Hogg?"

"It's not like those kids are black."

"Yeah, but you are. You can't get involved with the police here, Magna."

"Sometimes I really hate it when you use my name," she said.

Even with the pillow over her head, she heard the strains of a song she had loved lifetimes ago at college parties in West Philadelphia. Back then it had seemed that Ice Cube's defection from the West Coast to the Bomb Squad could unite all of black America—but now a white-girl voice started proudly yelling along:

Fuck you, Ice Cube!

Yeah, ha ha! It's the nigga you love to hate!

Magna snapped on her bedside lamp and looked at Jamal. Even without sitting up, he nodded. *Release the hounds.*

"Do you want to leave your name?" the operator had asked.

"I'd rather not," Magna had said.

As she hung up, she wondered if not leaving her name meant that the complaint wouldn't be registered, but a few minutes later, she and Jamal heard the approach of the cruiser beneath the hooting students, then the click of police shoes on gravel. Instinctively, Magna shut off the light again. Those kids sure had been surprised, listening *again* to "The Nigga You Love to Hate." She and Jamal had clung together, that night's argument now over, in her last, best memory of him. They used each other's bodies to stifle their laughter, though of course no one would have heard them. In the morning they awoke and laughed some more.

It didn't sound like anyone was arrested that night, hauled off from the party to the small Southern police station. Magna imagined she would be going there now. This had been a long time coming, maybe her whole life.

"Do you want to leave your name?" the operator asked now.

"Oh, I'll be here."

Against the advice she'd always heard (advice she'd never imagined being useful to her, like "Stop, drop and roll" or "Never let them take you to a second location"), Magna moved the accident victim, shifting him so that his head was now on her thigh. Using his name, she told him he would be okay. His eyes began to flutter, which alarmed her. Gently, she ordered him to stay awake. She could see him struggling with his eyelids; his gaze became glassy, then it focused on her with otherworldly calm. The calm of a sated baby, or, Magna supposed, someone giving in to death.

Back when Jamal was with her there in the town, Magna had made judicious use of the campus gym, climbing, pedaling furiously, and running nowhere. So the thigh was not quite a pillow, but was frankly headed there, full of human warmth between the boy's sweat-soaked, dark, curly head and the cold, hard street.

THE BONE WARD

BY KATE FOLK

BY NIGHT OUR BONES dissolve into our blood like sugar in tea. We sleep in antigravity pods with slick outer shells and vinyl interiors, our limbs held by Velcro straps, our torsos bound by cuirasses that force our lungs to expand. Classical music pipes through speakers, masking the ventilators' hum. Outside, coyotes range over the Montana plains, scratching and whining, searching for dead things to eat. As the sun rises, our skeletons stitch themselves back together.

Since my arrival four months ago, I've been the only woman on the Bone Ward. With me are Frankie, a tattooed Porsche mechanic from Oakland; Rick, a bald, portly man who owns a chain of grocery stores in central Florida; Tim, a wheaten-haired twenty-year-old who grew up on an Idaho farm; and Bradley, my love, the only one who matters. Bradley is a musician, tall with jewel-green eyes, long fingers, and lush, dark hair.

He is my conception of the perfect man, as if manifested through years of consolatory fantasies. When our eyes meet across the dining table or the TV room, my heart wrings itself out, flushing my extremities with blood heat.

The Bone Ward belongs to a loose collective of quarantines for esoteric diseases. Before I came, Bradley was seeing a woman in the Epidermal Ward, half a mile across the arid, crumbly land pocked with juniper and salt bush. Her skin was zebra-striped, the dark bands tender as deep bruises. Once, when they tried to have sex, Bradley grazed a dark stripe and she screamed, alerting the orderlies to his presence.

"I like that I can touch you wherever I want," Bradley said the first time we had sex. I lay on crinkling butcher paper in an exam room. He ran his hands over my body, thumbs pressing hard into my flesh.

The cause of total nocturnal bone loss remains a mystery. On the day I arrived, the men questioned me, trying to find a common thread in our stories that might explain why we'd developed TNBL. We could find no obvious link. There is no cure yet, but Dr. Will's treatment regimen has enabled the afflicted to lead relatively normal lives. Two patients have been discharged from the Bone Ward so far; I'll likely be the third. My bones now stay nearly solid through the night, and Dr. Will believes I'll be ready to go home in another month or two. But I'm in no hurry to return to my life in New York. I dread returning to my copywriting job at a slick Midtown ad agency, where I use my degree in English literature to hawk creams, gels, and cosmetic procedures to insecure women. I dread returning to my rituals of maintenance and control—the keto dieting and master cleanses, the Bikram yoga and SoulCycle, the monthly clockwork of organic facials and gel manicures and Brazilian waxes.

I dread, most of all, the happy hours and dinner parties with casual girlfriends, nights of fatalistic bonding over the dearth of good single men as we push deeper into our thirties. My secret hope is to leave the ward with Bradley, and he is at least a few months behind me, in the scheme of recovery. Thus, I've been stalling, treating my body carelessly and skipping the occasional dose of bone-girding meds, so that I won't be forced to leave before properly securing Bradley's love.

Today is my 124th day on the ward. I lie in my pod, inhaling the last wisps of morphine fog, and push the call button so our nurse, Ming, knows I'm awake. A new patient is scheduled to arrive today—a woman, Ming told us. I look forward to no longer being the sole locus of the men's desire for sex and nurturance and everything else women are to men. But a small, childish part of me feels possessive, as if these men belong to me. Part of me hopes the new woman will be unviable in some way—old or deformed or happily married.

"Morning," Ming says, lifting the top hatch of my pod. Ming is the sole nurse on the ward. She lives in Billings and drives in each morning before dawn, to be on hand when we wake in our pods. Though she's only in her mid-forties, she's become like a mother to all of us. She runs her hands under my body, peeling my sticky flesh from the upholstery. My thin cotton pajamas are soaked through with the fluids of reconstitution. Ming takes my elbow and helps me out of the pod. We go to an exam room, where she massages the skin over my bones, smoothing my skeleton into alignment. She measures my pelvis and reports that it's crooked by a few centimeters.

"You need to take it easy," she says, and I know she's referring to my trysts with Bradley. Last night we had sex in this exam room. My gaze drifts over the locked drawers of needles and gauze and I remember how I held the handles, my body folded at the waist, while Bradley's fingers gripped my hip bones, leaving faint bruises like smudges of ash.

Ming's concern is justified. Our bones grow increasingly pliable as night deepens, and strenuous activity near bedtime can throw our skeletons out of whack. In a worst-case scenario, my body could be damaged enough to necessitate a stint in the Iron Skeleton. I promise Ming I'll be more careful. She nods sternly, and discharges me to the women's shower room, where I wash and put on a fresh set of scrubs. I go to the kitchen, make coffee, and pour it into white mugs on which we've written our names in Sharpie. I know how each man likes his coffee, and I have the mugs ready for them on the table as they straggle in, one by one. Bradley's hair is tousled, his eyes puffy. When he sees me, he smiles and comes over to kiss my cheek before he takes his seat at the table.

For breakfast, we eat bran flakes in whole milk, fortified orange juice, and planks of walnut bread slathered with nutritive paste. Later, the men will be in high spirits, making crass jokes about getting boned and deboned. It never seems to get old. Frankie has invented bone-related nicknames for everyone: Tenderman, Chicken Nugget, Marshmallow Dick. When I arrived, he christened me Gumdrop, which has stuck as the others' nicknames haven't; at this point, I wonder whether the men even remember my real name.

For now, though, the men are silent, navigating waves of nausea and pain as their tendons and ligaments wrap and firm around new bone. I take small bites of walnut bread, averting my gaze from their downturned faces. Bradley places his hand on my thigh. We leave our cereal unfinished and head to a disused exam room at the far end of the corridor. Bradley runs his hands under the starched cotton of my V-neck top. He undoes the drawstring at my waist. We flatten the exam chair to horizontal. It's narrow, and we have to squeeze to fit, Bradley tucked behind me, molding his body to mine. His cock firms against my ass. I reach around and grip him until he comes.

I rinse my hand in the sink, catching a slice of my face in the metal towel dispenser. My eyes and skin are bright, my body vivid. I look five years younger than I did when I came to the Bone Ward.

"Thanks," Bradley says, with ironic casualness.

"No problem," I say, mirroring his tone.

"I'll get you back tonight. Don't feel up to it at the moment."

"Sure thing," I say. I sit beside him on the chair and rest my head on his shoulder, our feet dangling above the floor in matching canvas slippers.

We emerge into the corridor. The ward is shaped like a horseshoe. At the end of its arms sit the two Iron Skeletons, sleek black tubes seven feet long, the sides riddled with buttons and gauges and a panel that slides back to reveal the face of the patient inside. Most days, though, the Skeletons stand empty. They are a last resort, used in the most acute phases of the disease, or in the rare instance when our bones emerge from the night wrongly baked. Inside, highly pressurized air pumps the skeleton back into alignment, over the course of hours or days. It is a brutal process. I've never had to go there, but Bradley says it's torture.

The ward attendant, Sam, passes us, pushing a yellow janitor's bucket.

"Hi, Sam!" Bradley says, with mocking cheer. Sam scowls and keeps moving. Ming is the only real nurse here. Sam does maintenance on the ward. He cleans and restocks and hoists our bodies into the pods on nights when we wait too long to strap in. He wears a surgical mask on the ward at all times, though there is no evidence that TNBL is contagious.

Bradley and I head to the TV room, where the bulk of our day will be spent, waiting for Dr. Will to call us in one at a time to draw our blood, take X-rays, and measure our bone density. As usual, we watch *Maury* at three. Today is a paternity-test episode. A young, blonde woman named Amy is back for a second round, having brought another contemptuous man who insists he's not the father of her baby. A looped video of the infant appears on a screen behind them. It crawls around a studio crib, its pudgy fingers grasping for off-camera toys. The audience coos on the first few loops, but the baby's evocative power soon fades and the crowd trains its fervor on the man, JC, who sports a goatee and an oversize Billabong T-shirt.

Bradley and I sit on the loveseat, my legs slung over his lap. I straighten and grab his hand when it's time for Maury to reveal the results of the paternity test, as though it were the final, climactic moment of a sporting event.

"I bet he's the dad," Tim says—sweet, young Tim, who was struck down by TNBL just before he was heading to Indiana on a basketball scholarship. "The baby looks like him."

"The baby looks the same as all babies," Frankie says grumpily. He leans back in his chair, muscular arms crossed over his chest. Frankie's arms are covered in tattoos, intricate patchworks of diamonds, flames, a dagger, a bird's outstretched wing. I've always wondered what his arms look like at night, the images distorted by the stretched canvas of his boneless flesh.

"What are you talking about?" Tim insists. "There's totally a resemblance."

Rick shushes them; he's sitting forward in his chair, elbows on knees, his broad back humped in a manner that would earn Ming's disapproval. Bradley and I exchange a smile, amused by how engaged the men are in Amy's saga. Though of course we are too.

"JC," Maury says, pausing for suspense, "you are *not* the father."

JC leaps from his chair, whooping and unleashing a string of joyful, bleeped expletives at Amy, Maury, and the studio audience. In the TV room, the men chuckle, presumably at Amy's impressive promiscuity. I find myself laughing, too, at the ridiculous scene of JC taunting the crowd, though in my previous life I would have found the show revolting.

Beneath the riotous sounds of the studio audience, we hear the front doors of the ward open. Tim mutes the TV and we listen to Ming giving the new patient a tour. A female voice responds with murmurs of understanding and assent to Ming's descriptions of how the ward operates, the measures we are expected to take to ensure our own survival. Bradley's hand is warm in mine. I give it a squeeze.

Ming and the new patient enter the TV room. She's cut from the cloth of my nightmares: petite, with wide hazel eyes, caramel-colored hair, bangs low across her forehead. Her arms and legs are delicate, milky stems protruding from the silken edges of a blue polka-dotted dress. She wears no makeup, no jewelry, no polish on her nails. My career writing ad copy to exploit women's physical insecurities has rendered me expert in the minutiae of female beauty. In this sense, I am like a judge of pedigree dogs, or horses. When I say that this woman is flawless, I do not mean it lightly. She possesses no attribute that I would, in good faith, suggest augmenting or reducing, highlighting or minimizing, smoothing or shaping or lengthening or rejuvenating or otherwise subjecting to any of the countless verbs I employed daily to describe the infinite ways in which a woman might fail to achieve her corporeal potential. I would not know how to sell her a thing.

The new woman stands in front of us and waves. "Hi. I'm Olivia," she chirps.

The air of the ward ripples. The men stare at Olivia with a predatory hunger that turns my stomach; how obvious and crude it looks, when directed at someone else. They each stand and introduce themselves with a gallantry I find comical, given their usual behavior. Bradley removes his hand from mine and wipes his palm on the loveseat's upholstery before shaking Olivia's hand. He then offers her his seat.

"Hi," she says, settling in next to me.

Her palm is cool and dry. Even up close, the skin of her face appears poreless. When she crosses her legs, I smell baby powder and SPF moisturizer.

The men watch Olivia with furtive curiosity. They ask gentle questions. With every answer, she reveals herself to be even more threatening than I had feared. Olivia comes from a small town in Tennessee. Since graduating from college, she's worked as an outreach coordinator for a domestic violence shelter. She is twenty-six, the daughter of a preacher and a seamstress. She grew up singing gospel music in the Baptist church, and spent the previous summer touring the South with her cousin's bluegrass band.

"Sing us something, sweetheart," Frankie says, his voice uncharacteristically soft.

"Oh, no, I'd be too embarrassed," Olivia says.

"Come on," Tim whines.

"Please," Bradley adds softly.

Olivia clears her throat and begins singing "Amazing Grace." My eyes tear with embarrassment for her—how cliché. But the men are rapt. Her voice is surprisingly rich and powerful, incongruous with her tiny frame. When she finishes, they applaud.

"We'll call her Starling," Frankie says.

"Our little songbird," Rick agrees.

It quickly becomes clear that Olivia is sicker than any of us were when we came to the ward. Her slim fingers are arthritic, their joints bulbous. She walks with a careful limp. At dinner, her face is tense. She does not speak. I feel terrible for her; she must be in extraordinary pain.

"You should eat something, Starling," Frankie says.

Olivia shakes her head. "It's okay," she says. "I'm not feeling well."

"The food is calibrated to our bodies' needs," Bradley says, like a Boy Scout reciting survival tips. "It'll do you good."

Tim spreads marrow on Olivia's bread and offers it to her. Olivia looks like she will cry. She raises the bread to her mouth and takes a tiny bite. Her face pales. She gags, a milky spittle pushing past her lips. She tries to gather it all in a napkin.

Bradley calls for help. Ming runs over; Sam brings the wheelchair. They lower Olivia's rubbery body into the chair. I am astonished. Her bone loss has started already, and it's not even 6:00 p.m. We watch her skeleton melt with alarming speed. Sam touches her upper arm and his glove comes away sticky with calcium sap, a by-product of bone dissolution. Her face sags into a leering putty mask. Her head droops on the wilting stem of her spine. I avert my eyes, feeling nauseous.

Olivia is wheeled off to the Iron Skeleton. We sit in embarrassed silence, as if we'd accidentally witnessed something private.

"Jeez," Tim says. "That was nuts."

"Poor girl," Rick says, shaking his head.

"I wouldn't wish the Iron Skeleton on my worst enemy," Bradley says.

After dinner, Bradley and I huddle on the bench in the courtyard, surrounded by denuded trees and the planters of wildflowers that we take turns plucking weeds from. Before succumbing to TNBL, Bradley was principal cellist in the Chicago Symphony Orchestra. Today he received another get-well card from members of his section. Bradley hasn't seen any of them since last summer's concert, from which he was removed on a stretcher. The cellos were playing their solo in the largo movement of Dvořák's *New World Symphony* when the fingers of Bradley's left hand crumpled, his bow belching a granular, open-stringed C before clattering to the floor. The concert was halted. The audience watched, horrified, as Bradley's body melted, arms splaying, head rolling back, mouth gaping up at the rigging of stage lights.

"They never tell me anything real," Bradley says. "It's always like, *We're thinking of you and can't wait to have you back*. That's bullshit. I'm sure they're well into the auditioning process for a new principal by now."

"I'm sorry," I say. "But if they do end up replacing you, you'll find something else. Any orchestra would be lucky to have you."

"Yeah, but a principal position in a major symphony isn't something you land every day," Bradley says, a bit testily.

It was Bradley who proposed that the ward play music while our bones dissolve. He arranged a soothing mix of Bach, Debussy, Chopin. Over the past three months, Bradley has taught me to love classical music. At night we listen to Stravinsky and Tchaikovsky and Beethoven on a battered CD player. A few times, I've tried reading to him from the two books of poetry I brought with me, Neruda and Dickinson, but as soon as I begin a poem, Bradley's eyes glaze over, and I know I am boring him.

"Olivia seems nice," I say, to change the subject.

"Yeah," Bradley says. "Poor thing."

"I remember how disoriented I was when I first got here," I say. I had wound up on the ward suddenly, after dismissing my worsening symptoms for months, attributing them variously to hangovers, seasonal flus, a proliferation of candida in my gut. Some days I walked with a limp; others, I had to pouf my hair to cover a dent in my skull. Finally, on a Saturday night in December, I brought a man home from a bar in Murray Hill. He worked in finance, a cherubic, pale-eyed blond. In the morning I woke in a pool of fluid that I mistook for urine. I now know it was the excretion of bone loss. The banker was sitting at the end of the bed, staring at me. He asked what was wrong with my face. I had slept on my stomach, my face pressed into the mattress. I raised my fingers to find my nose flattened against my cheeks. My left shoulder had been wrenched from its socket, arm dangling outward. My left hand was gnarled from where it had lain on reconstitution, crushed under the weight of my hip. The fingers jutted at wild angles, like the arms of a Joshua tree. In the emergency room, a bewildered young doctor called the CDC, and by evening I was on a flight to Billings, bound for the Bone Ward.

I've withheld this story from Bradley, worrying he'd be turned off by the part about me fucking a man I'd met at a bar the same night. I want to tell him now, though; he's made himself vulnerable, telling me about his fears of being replaced, and I have the urge to reciprocate.

But Bradley preempts me. "I can't wait to get out of this fucking place," he says. "Dr. Will says it should only be a few more months."

"That's great," I say, forcing the words around the ache in my chest. I feel betrayed whenever Bradley talks about leaving. "What do you think you'll do next?"

Bradley stares across the courtyard. I know he's choosing his words carefully.

"Who knows what'll happen," he says. "Maybe I'll get a job in New York."

It is the closest he's gotten to suggesting a life together outside of the ward. "That would be great," I say, aiming for a breezy tone.

Bradley chucks me on the arm. "Come on, Gumdrop," he says. "I owe you an orgasm."

We bring the CD player into an exam room and Bradley puts on Rachmaninoff's Piano Concerto no. 2. Amid the moody interplay of piano and strings, Bradley uses his mouth and fingers to make me come. I then help him climb into his pod. I position the ventilator over his mouth, strap on his cuirass, and watch as the rippled tubes raise the wall of his chest. His green eyes gaze up at me in the moment before I lower the lid, sealing him in for the night.

I climb into my own pod, though it will be hours before my bones soften. Dr. Will told me I don't need to use the ventilator anymore. I sometimes miss the sensation of total bone loss, its own kind of orgasm. A forced surrender, a sudden lack—like a floor dropping out, air and light rushing into a room.

For three days, Olivia is confined to the Skeleton. On the third afternoon, we're sitting in the TV room watching *Judge Joe Brown* when a wheelchair squeaks behind us. Sam wheels Olivia over and parks her next to me.

"Thank you, Sam," Olivia says. Sam blushes and slinks away.

Olivia trains her sweetness on me. "How are you feeling today?" she asks.

"I'm fine," I say, both irritated and charmed by her kindness.

"How are *you* feeling?" Tim asks Olivia.

"Oh, I've been worse," Olivia said. "You all know how it is."

Once again, Olivia's presence seems to have displaced the air in the room. I catch Bradley sneaking looks at her. He keeps a few inches of distance between us on the couch.

Ming walks back into the TV room. "I forgot to tell you, dear," she says to Olivia. "You've received some packages."

"My guitar?" Olivia says, perking up.

"Among other things. You're a popular lady."

Olivia shrugs, self-effacingly. "It's probably all from people in my dad's congregation," she says. "I've asked him a million times to keep me out of his sermons, but he can't help himself. Especially now, I'm sure."

Ming nods. "Well, it's stacked in the entryway, whenever you want to take a look."

"You want to go now, Starling?" Frankie says, after Ming leaves.

"Not right now, I don't think," Olivia says. "I'm pretty exhausted."

"You play guitar?" Bradley says.

"I did," Olivia says. "I don't think I'll be able to anymore, though. Not for a while."

"Will you teach me?" Bradley says. His tone is playful, but I know he's serious.

"Sure," Olivia says, beaming. "I'd love to."

It's my night to cook dinner. I prepare a meal from Dr. Will's binder of recipes. I scramble eggs, grind the shells with a pestle and sprinkle them into sautéed spinach. I assemble a spread of white cheddar, flaxseed crackers, marrow, and sardines in olive oil. I fill our mugs with warm bone broth, selecting an unmarked mug for Olivia from the cabinet. I consider writing her name on it, but decide not to. I know she would lavish me with gratitude for such a gesture, and the prospect embarrasses me. If she wants to claim a mug, she can ask.

I ferry the food from kitchen to table. The men coo in a parody of appreciation, and I am reassured that nothing has changed.

"Your hair looks nice that way, Gumdrop," Tim says. Before cooking, I had pulled my hair into a bun.

"Like a ballerina," Rick adds.

"Very pretty," Olivia agrees, and I blush; her praise carries more weight than the men's, as her tone is so earnest.

We eat.

"The spinach is good tonight, Gumdrop," Frankie says. "Lots of lemon. Just how I like it."

"She's a good cook," Bradley says, and I blush again.

"She'd be prettier if she smiled, though," Frankie teases, as he does every night. In response, I roll my eyes and make a point of frowning.

"What about you, Starling?" Rick says, blushing as he looks at Olivia. "Will you give us a smile?"

It's a joke, because Olivia is already grinning. "You're all too much," she says with a laugh. "Leave us poor girls alone."

The night is warm, and Tim proposes shooting hoops in the courtyard before dark. It's Bradley's night to do the dishes, but I see that he wants to go. I tell him I'll take his shift.

"Are you sure?" Bradley says.

"Yep," I say, patting him on the thigh.

"I'll pick up your Thursday shift," he says, and I nod, already knowing that he'll forget, and that I won't remind him.

When the others leave, Olivia and Rick remain seated, having fallen into an intense, private conversation. I ferry plates to the kitchen while Rick tells Olivia about his wife, who left him after the onset of TNBL. Rick's wife was repulsed by his illness, the acrid smell released by the dissolution of bone, the fluid pooled under him when he woke. She believed these were symptoms of a sexually transmitted disease, which gave her a pretext to leave him.

I've avoided Rick as if his gloom were a contagion, while Olivia sits with him long after dinner, asking questions, encouraging him to pour out the dregs of his heart. I stand near the door, keeping the water at a low pitch so I can hear Olivia's softly reassuring voice.

"That's so unfair," she tells Rick. "I'm sorry you've had to go through all that." I feel guilty now for never taking the time to listen to Rick. I have been wholly focused on Bradley, and I wonder if the other men have resented me for it.

I clear Rick and Olivia's plates from the table last, not wanting to interrupt their conversation.

"Thank you," Olivia says, when I take her plate. Her face tilts up at me like a sunflower. I curve my lips in a toothless smile. I scrub pots until my fingers blanch and peel.

The next day Olivia is well enough to sit with us in the TV room. *Maury* is showing another paternity episode: Amy's back for a third round. The man she's brought today is younger than the others. He is skinny, with buzzed hair and crusts of healing acne in the hollows of his cheeks. His face rests in a sneer.

Olivia and I sit on the loveseat, the men perched on folding chairs in a semicircle around us. "Tyler," Maury intones, "you are *not* the father." Tyler jumps up from his chair and does a touchdown dance on the stage. The crowd erupts. In the TV room, the men snicker, as usual. Tim and Frankie high-five, as if a part of this hateful victory belonged to them.

"This show is disgusting," Olivia says softly. She leaves the room.

The men fall silent, chastened. I've thought the same thing many times about *Maury* but have kept this opinion to myself, because I enjoyed our collective indulgence in trashy TV shows. We continue watching, but the mood has soured. At the next commercial break, Bradley gets up and leaves without a word. I assume he's gone to the bathroom, but when he doesn't come back after twenty minutes, I go looking. Through the hall window, I see him sitting with Olivia on the bench in the courtyard. I stand by the window, listening to her sing a jazzy version of "Swing Low, Sweet Chariot." While she sings, Bradley keeps the beat with finger snaps.

The next afternoon, Bradley eschews TV again in order to sit with Olivia in the courtyard. During the quiet parts of the shows, we can hear him picking out melodies on Olivia's guitar.

This pattern persists all week. Bradley and I continue having sex in the mornings. He still greets me affectionately, and sits next to me during meals. But he spends more and more of his free time with Olivia, in the courtyard. Sometimes when I pass by the window, I see Bradley holding the guitar awkwardly while Olivia coaxes his cello-calloused fingers into the proper configurations. Other times, she's singing while Bradley jots notes in his Moleskine notebook. But often, they are simply sitting and talking, as Bradley and I used to do.

One night at dinner, Bradley and Olivia announce that they've begun collaborating on a music project. They're both excited, aglow with creative adrenaline; my chest aches with jealousy, though I pretend to be happy for them.

I stop Bradley as he exits the dining room.

"We never spend time together anymore," I say, wincing at how I sound—like a nagging, needy girlfriend.

Bradley sighs, as if he's known he would have to submit to this conversation at some point but has been avoiding it. He explains that it's the first time in months that he's felt artistically fulfilled; that it's the most fundamental part of his identity, and only now does he realize how depressed he's been without making music.

I nod numbly. "I'm glad you're feeling inspired," I say. I can't quite rid my voice of hurt, but he doesn't seem to register it.

"Thanks," he says, beaming at me. "I think you're really going to dig what we're working on. It's a lot more innovative than what I'm used to. Obviously." He laughs.

"Edgier than Mozart," I say.

"Something like that."

I am trying not to cry. Bradley finally notices I'm upset. "Aw, come on, Gumdrop," he says, drawing me in for a hug. "We've gotta work again tonight, but I'll swing by later and see what you're up to."

Bradley joins me and Tim in the TV room around 9:00 p.m., presumably after strapping Olivia into her pod. We're watching an old John Cusack movie from the ward's DVD collection. Bradley sits beside me on the couch. He slings his arm around my shoulder, but his posture is stiff, his leg tapping with restless energy. I have rarely felt a person's absence so acutely.

Another week passes. At breakfast one morning, I realize Bradley and I haven't had sex in five days. Later, while he's washing dishes, I take his hand and pull him into the bathroom attached to the kitchen. We have sex quickly, impersonally, while standing. After he comes, Bradley will barely look at me. He wipes his penis on a paper towel, then pulls up his scrubs and goes to the sink to wash his hands, as if to erase any trace of me.

"What's wrong?" I say.

"Nothing," Bradley says, turning suddenly, as if he'd forgotten I'm here. "What do you mean?"

"You're in love with her, aren't you?" I say impulsively.

Bradley gives me a look he's never given me before—a side-glance of contempt I remember from previous boyfriends, at the start of a long unraveling.

"We've been over this," Bradley says. "Nothing has changed. I've just been focused on this project. I'm really excited about it. I hoped you'd be happy for me."

"I am," I say. "Of course. But what about me, Bradley?"

Bradley pauses. "I don't think I'm in a position right now to be responsible for anyone else's needs," he says coolly. "This isn't exactly an environment that's conducive to a serious relationship. I assumed that was obvious."

"Who said anything about a serious relationship?" I say, floundering.

"Well, that's what it sounds like," Bradley says. He pulls another towel from the dispenser and begins drying his hands. "Listen, Gumdrop. You know I enjoy spending time with you. But I just can't deal with this kind of pressure right now."

"I'm sorry," I say, cringing at how desperate I sound. "I didn't mean to pressure you."

But it's too late. Bradley throws the wadded towel in the trash and moves to the door. "I think maybe it's best if we cool it for a little while," he says. "At least until the album is done."

After Bradley and I separate, the other men seem to withdraw from me as well. Frankie no longer bothers asking me to smile. At dinner each night, he says, "Hey, Starling, you're prettier when you smile," and Olivia looks at him and flashes a giant smile. Her joke is an inversion of mine, complying where I had refused. One night, I snap. When Frankie says his dumb line and Olivia smiles, on cue, like a well-trained dog, I say, "She's pretty whether she smiles or not."

I feel the men bristle against me. Olivia giggles and places her dry hand on mine.

"It's okay, hon," she says. "Frankie doesn't mean it that way."

We finish our food in silence. Later that night, I stand in the darkened hall, watching as Bradley sits next to Olivia's pod. He reads to her from a book of Whitman's poems she brought in her floral-print duffel. He's placed the CD player at his feet, and I can just make out the Rachmaninoff suite unspooling beneath his ridiculous poetry-voice.

Tim and I watch a horror movie in the TV room—one in which a meagerly clothed woman runs through a forest, chased by a murderer, her cleavage smeared with blood. I watch the scenes of gore with dull eyes, the screen of my mind retaining the image of Bradley by Olivia's pod. I had considered Rachmaninoff significant to our relationship—it was Bradley's go-to accompaniment for sex—but he has repurposed our song as if it meant nothing. A few weeks ago, this would have wounded me, but I feel eerily calm. The feared thing has already happened, and I am now able to spectate on the particulars of my own rejection as if from a slight remove. It is a relief to no longer have something to lose.

Tim's bones begin to soften and he's forced to return to his pod before the movie ends. I wait for the credits to roll, then stand and stretch. It's 11:00 p.m. and my bones are still firm. I could leave the ward tomorrow, go back to New York. But that would mean giving up on Bradley completely. Though my rational mind tells me it's hopeless, my heart clings to contradictory evidence—Bradley's insistence that there is nothing romantic between him and Olivia, and his promise to reevaluate our relationship once the album is finished. There is hope for us, my heart insists, as long as I remain on the ward.

Aside from the hum of the machinery that enables us to survive the night, the ward is silent; Sam is probably outside smoking, or asleep on his cot in the break room. I must pass Olivia's pod on the way to my own. The instant the idea occurs to me, my body reacts, as if it had been preparing itself. Suddenly I am moving to the back of Olivia's pod and pulling the plug that powers the antigravity in one quick motion, like tearing a root from the earth. Immediately, I regret it; there is not even a moment of satisfaction, only horror at the damage I might have caused. The antigravity keeps everything in place; without it, the pressure on her organs could kill her immediately. I bend down and grab at the cord, but it's fallen into a gap between the pod and the wall. Ten seconds pass before I can get the plug back in. I feel the whoosh of the antigravity powering up, and exhale. Above me, Debussy ends and Bach begins. I crawl into my pod and strap myself in for the night.

*　　*　　*

By 10:00 a.m., Olivia still hasn't pressed the call button. Ming raps on the lid.

"Olivia, you awake?" she says.

We gather and wait for Olivia's response, but the pod remains silent. My chest floods with dread. Olivia's bones must have been pure liquid when I unplugged her pod.

I try to reassure myself. At least I did nothing to interfere with the ventilator, which runs on a separate power source, and the lapse was brief—fifteen seconds at most. Still, fifteen seconds is an eternity at the nadir of bonelessness.

Ming presses the manual release and the lid shudders up. She shoos us back, but not before I catch a glimpse of Olivia. She is a pile of flesh without human form, rippled like caramel dripped from a spoon. Her skull forms an ellipse. One eye has rolled back into her head. The other stares straight ahead from a slacken socket. The whole heap of her is wet looking, like cheese left out to sweat in the sun.

Sam carries Olivia to an exam room. I go to the courtyard and sit on a bench. I pick at my cuticles, my mind fogged with terror that the others will discover my crime. I know that with each passing minute, the likelihood that I will confess diminishes. The time to do so was last night, as soon as I replaced the plug, when perhaps some of the damage to Olivia's body could have been mitigated.

Tim comes out after a few minutes and kneels beside the wildflower plot.

"Ming thinks Olivia must have skipped a dose of her meds," Tim says, his back to me. "She can't talk. There might be brain damage."

"That's awful," I say, genuinely horrified. I wish he would stop talking.

"They think it's weird that she would suddenly get so much worse. She was improving."

"Who knows, with this disease?" I say.

"It's weird, is all I'm saying." He's gathered a pile of flowers at his knee.

"What are you doing?" I say.

"We're making a garland for Olivia's pod," Tim says. "So when she comes back, she'll know we've been thinking about her."

I wonder whose idea it was. I wonder if Bradley proposed it, while they huddled in the corridor outside the Skeleton. I wonder if he would do the same for me.

Rick comes out. He takes a handful of wildflowers and sits beside me on the bench. He puts on his reading glasses and begins tying dental floss around the stems of the flowers. I consider offering to help, but I sense their project has no space for me. I go back inside, where Olivia's pod stands open like a display casket. The vinyl gleams, still slick with fluid; Sam hasn't yet had a chance to wipe it down.

Today, Bradley joins the rest of us in the TV room. He hesitates for a moment before sitting next to me on the loveseat. He glances at me with a perfunctory smile, then turns his attention to the TV.

Amy is back on *Maury* for the fourth time. This time she's brought a man in his forties with tattoos and a wet-looking ponytail. He slouches in his seat, legs splayed wide, with an attitude of profound boredom.

"Arturo, you *are* the father," Maury announces. The crowd erupts. Arturo's knee jiggles. He smiles and shrugs as if this had happened to him many times before. Bradley leaves the TV room, the studio audience clamoring in his wake.

"She's going to be okay," I say, meaning Olivia—though I have no basis for this conclusion.

"Like you care," Frankie says. He gets up and follows Bradley to the courtyard to help with Olivia's garland. I watch Arturo mumble amiably through an interview. The baby is brought out and placed in his arms. He looks at it in the grim yet resolute way a man might look at a part of his roof that has caved in, necessitating expensive repairs. It is clear he will be an absent, indifferent father, but for now everyone is satisfied that the mystery has been solved.

At breakfast the next morning, Bradley says we should go visit Olivia in the Skeleton. I point out that she won't be able to hear us in there, but the men look at me with disgust and say that isn't the point.

Ming stands before the Skeleton with a clipboard, jotting notes on Olivia's vitals. A heart-rate monitor steadily beeps. The apparatus hums, red and green lights flashing. Ming slides back the panel, exposing a smoky pane of glass at the level of Olivia's head. The men take turns crouching down. They wave and speak loudly, saying they miss her and hope she'll be back with us soon. When it's my turn, Olivia's eyes regard me with calm intelligence. Fear grips my throat. For the first time, I realize Olivia might have been awake when I unplugged her pod. She would not have heard me approach, due to the hum of the ventilator, but she would have felt the anti-gravity shut off, and then lurch back on. It could not have been an outage; the ward's backup generators are configured to prevent even a momentary lapse. The only conclusion would have been that someone had unplugged her pod, and I am the only patient capable of moving in the middle of the night.

"Hi, Olivia," I say. Her eyelids slowly shutter, dismissing me.

The others wander back to the TV room. I go for a walk, hoping to calm my nerves. It's a warm day, violently bright. I slowly circle the perimeter of the Bone Ward. To the west, the mountains of Custer Gallatin National Forest rise in felted ridges. To the north, I can just make out the converted red barn that houses the Epidermal Ward. Beyond that, stacked on a hill, sit the low white barracks of the Hirsute Ward. I circle back to the front of the Bone Ward, which faces east. I squint down the road that runs unpaved, wheel ruts pressed into dirt, for five miles before intersecting with Highway 212, which leads to Billings. I could call a cab and escape before my crime is discovered. But I need to clear my release with Dr. Will. I need prescriptions and a plan for continued treatment. Without medication, my progress will quickly come undone.

I enter the ward, eyes aching against the sudden dark. I hear the low murmur of voices in the TV room. As I approach, the men shudder into silence.

"What?" I say.

No one will make eye contact. I know they've been talking about me.

During a commercial break, I follow Bradley to the kitchen. He flips the switch of the electric kettle.

"What's up with you guys?" I say.

"Nothing," he says.

"Come on, Bradley," I say. "What's going on?"

Bradley does not look at me. He peels open the foil envelope of a tea bag.

"We were just talking about how weird it is that Olivia got so much worse all of a sudden."

My stomach folds. I nod, playing along. "It's strange," I say. "But relapses can happen with diseases like this."

"Dr. Will says he's never seen it."

"Well, he doesn't have a huge body of evidence to draw from, does he?"

The kettle rattles. Bradley pours water into his mug.

"Your bones are back to normal," Bradley says. "Why don't you go home?"

I watch him slowly bob the tea bag, its string coiled around two fingers, as if he had not just broken my heart again.

"You want me to leave?" I say.

"I find it strange that you don't want to."

"I do want to," I say. "I'm just not strong enough yet."

"Sam says you've been staying up later and later."

I pause. "Why were you talking about me to Sam?"

Bradley shrugs. He lifts the dripping tea bag and drops it into the trash before it's had a chance to steep.

To absolve myself, I must regress. I must hitch myself to Olivia, becoming another patient whose progress has inexplicably reversed. I stop taking the medications doled out with breakfast. I stash the big red pills along the inner seams of my pod.

I don't expect it to happen so quickly. My bones soften earlier each night, and I wake to the old pain of bone tunneling through flesh. One night I'm watching *Dateline NBC* after the others have gone to bed, and when I stand my legs crumple under me like wet cardboard. I lie on the tile until Sam finds me on his final rounds through the ward. He carries the soft mass of my body to my pod. He straps me in with quick, aggressive movements of his work-calloused hands, anxious to be done with me.

In the morning, I report to Dr. Will's office. Dr. Will is a lanky blond of indeterminate age, his face eerily smooth from Botox and retinoid creams. He's based in Los Angeles, at Cedars-Sinai, but committed to a year on the ward to further his research on TNBL. Dr. Will sits on his wheeled stool, thumbing through my charts and shaking his head.

"I don't get it," he says. "You were doing so well."

I feel guilty for skewing his data. I'm sicker than I was the day I arrived, five months ago, at the Bone Ward.

"The same thing happened to Olivia, didn't it?" I say carefully.

"Yes, but Olivia's TNBL was far more advanced than yours. Her condition has always been tenuous. But you! You were almost ready for discharge."

I'm relieved that Dr. Will doesn't seem to find Olivia's relapse suspicious. I nod along with his suggestions, his proposal to double my dosage. At the end of our meeting, I am confident enough to ask, "How is Olivia doing now, anyway?"

Dr. Will sighs and massages his temples; the subject clearly causes him grief. "Her condition is improving, but it'll be a long road. She should be out of the Skeleton soon, at least."

Fear dances up my spine. "And the damage?"

"From what I can tell, she's suffered a major setback. She won't be able to speak, at least for a while."

"How awful," I say, letting out a breath I didn't know I'd been holding.

A few days after my consultation with Dr. Will, Olivia is wheeled out for breakfast. Her eyes are dim, her mind seemingly numbed by painkillers and a triple dose of bone-girding meds. Her beauty has been chewed to a pulp: her face flattened, her lower eyelids sagging, her cheekbones fallen. Sam prepares for her a smoothie in place of solid food. Olivia uses her fingers to pinch her lips around the straw.

We try to pretend everything's the same as before. Frankie says, "Hey, Starling, let's see those pearly whites." Olivia slowly raises her face. Her eyes flare with determination. She attempts to hitch the rigging of her muscles into a smile, but her mouth cants at a grotesque diagonal. Her upper lip curls to expose a single eyetooth. The men force chuckles and murmurs of encouragement.

I can't bear to watch any more. I get up from the table and take my dish to the kitchen, exaggerating my new limp.

The next morning I wake later than everyone. Ming carefully unstraps me from the Velcro scaffold and peels the cuirass from my chest. I am too weak to stand. Sam and Ming lift me from the pod and wedge me into a wheelchair. The lights of the ward blur. I hear the clinking of forks on plates as I'm wheeled past the dining room. I can't turn my head to face them, but I know they are watching me.

The Skeleton wraps me in its purr. Needles of cold, highly pressurized air pulse into me, penetrating every millimeter of my skin. Even through the cloak of morphine, this pain is like nothing I've felt before. It is many magnitudes worse than the pain of reconstitution. It feels as if my skin had been peeled off and coarse salt rubbed into the open wound of my body. My mouth opens in a silent scream. The air is pumped with high doses of bone-girding medication, acrid clouds that sear my trachea. I remain awake, in agony, for hours that stretch into days.

Finally the Skeleton powers off. The hatch opens. Ming's face is drawn in apology.

"How you feeling, hon?" she says. I nod, my eyes welling with gratitude that the ordeal is over. I resolve to begin taking my medication again. Anything to avoid being sent back to the Skeleton.

Ming wheels me to the TV room. It appears to be late afternoon, the sun casting opaque wedges of light through the west-facing windows. The men stare at me. I adopt Olivia's old tactic of diverting attention from my pain to theirs.

"How are you feeling, Olivia?" I ask. Olivia is still in a wheelchair, her head slumped toward her left shoulder. Her lips bubble with saliva, as if in response. The men glance at Olivia, then avert their eyes. They seem relieved that I look the same as before, my body pumped back to recognizable form.

"Good to see you, Gumdrop," Frankie says. "You had us worried."

It is enough just to be out of the Skeleton, but it seems my plan has worked better than I'd hoped. During dinner, the men treat me like they used to, as though I have redeemed myself through suffering. Even Bradley looks at me again with fondness.

"It's good to have you back," he whispers, squeezing my hand under the table.

I begin taking my pills again, in excess of Dr. Will's increased dosage, drawing from the stash I've collected in the seams of my pod. I pray my progress will be quick, but after such an alarming relapse, I know Dr. Will won't sign off on my discharge until I've been stable at least a few weeks.

My time in the Skeleton has put things into perspective, exposing my obsession with Bradley as childish. I am now eager to leave the ward, to return to New York, as any sane person would have wanted to do months ago. When Bradley's attention pivots toward me again, I resist. I feel I do not deserve his affection, considering what it has driven me to do. I spend most of my days alone, reading in the courtyard and making contact with people back home, preparing myself for reentry.

But it does not take much for Bradley to wear down my resistance. One day, I'm reading Emily Dickinson in the courtyard when he comes out and joins me on the bench. I ignore him and keep reading for a few minutes, then give up, putting the book down.

Bradley takes my hand. He massages the joints and presses his lips to my knuckles. "I've missed you," he says, and I know he isn't referring only to my time in the Skeleton, but also to the weeks after Olivia came, when he chose her over me.

"I've missed you too," I say cautiously.

"I didn't appreciate what I had with you," he says. "I didn't treat you well. I'm sorry."

"It's okay," I say, feeling the ground shift beneath me.

In an exam room, I complete my surrender. Bradley presses his body to mine. He kisses the nape of my neck. His fingers press my pelvis and thighs, molding my supple bones into the shape of his desire. I taste his skin, wishing I could unhinge my jaw and swallow him whole. As we lie entwined, my back to his, I cry silently, because I know I will never have him. The other times I've been in love, there was hope of a future. With Bradley, I harbor no such illusions. I know we will not have a life together beyond the ward. What I feared from the beginning was confirmed in Olivia—that given a world of women to choose from, he will never, ever choose me.

Perhaps it is possible, though, to revise my idea of love. To remain in the present; to love Bradley now even though I know he will only hurt me in the end. But it doesn't really matter either way. I am too weak not to claim every moment with him that is offered.

When it's time to leave the exam room, I wipe my eyes so he won't see I've been crying. We've waited a bit too long, and my bones are weak. Bradley picks me up and carries me to my pod. Before he lowers the lid, he pauses to kiss my forehead, as I'd told him my mother used to do, when she tucked me in for the night.

One morning, three weeks after I resumed taking my meds, the men propose we go for a hike.

They're already gathered around the breakfast table when I enter the dining room, talking in hushed voices, so Ming won't hear.

"It's supposed to hit seventy this afternoon," Tim tells me, excitedly.

"Sounds nice," I say. "But what about Ming?"

"She's taking a half day," Rick says in a low voice. "Doctor's appointment in Billings."

"It's Dr. Will's day off too," Tim says. "We won't get another chance like this."

"I dunno," I say.

"Come on, Gumdrop," Frankie says. "You used to take walks all the time."

"I'm not as strong as I used to be."

Bradley rubs my thigh. "You should come," he says. "The vitamin D will do you good."

We pack lunches: thermoses of bone broth, kale chips, cartons of Greek yogurt. Around one, Ming comes into the TV room.

"I'll be back in the morning," she says. "Sam will be here in a few hours for the night shift. And Dr. Will is on call if anything happens."

"We're good, Ming Ming," Frankie says. "Go do what you gotta do."

We stand at the entrance and watch Ming's hatchback disappear over a hump in the rutted dirt road. For the first time in the six months I've been here, the Bone Ward is left unattended.

The sun is hot on my shoulders. We walk toward the base of the foothills, Frankie and Tim forging ahead, Bradley and me picking our way slowly over the scrub. Rick waddles alone between the two groups, the sun searing his bald patch.

We walk for over an hour.

"Bradley," I say, my breath coming short. "I need to rest."

We sit beside a juniper bush. Bradley has carried our lunches in a backpack. We drink water and bone broth. We share a Tupperware of limp kale chips. When we're done eating, we lie back and gaze into the dome of the sky.

The other men circle back, settle in beside us, and eat their own lunches. No one seems in any rush to return to the ward.

"Shouldn't we be heading back?" I say.

"In a minute," Bradley says.

"We want to watch the sunset," Frankie says.

I have lost track of time. When Frankie mentions the sunset, I sit up, alarmed, and see that the sun has begun its descent toward the mountains. My skin prickles with awareness. Once the sun is down, it will be too late. In another half hour my bones will be too weak to stand on.

"No," I say. "We have to go now."

"You go on ahead," Tim says.

"We're watching the sunset," Rick adds. Their voices are mechanical, as though they were reading from a script. I realize they must have been planning this for weeks. Perhaps Olivia confirmed their suspicions while I was in the Skeleton. Maybe she has learned to communicate through taps of her fingers, through saliva bubbles or blinks.

I rise to my feet, my body trembling. I try to run, but my legs buckle under me after two steps.

"Poor Gumdrop," Frankie says. "You should have remembered to take your pills." I look at him, stunned; for the first time, I realize how easily they could have found my stash of pills, those long days I was locked in the Skeleton.

The men get up. They stretch and yawn. So this is how it will happen—casually, their faces masked with benign smiles. They will murder me by walking away.

Bradley stands over me. I grasp his ankle with both hands.

"Please, Bradley," I say. "I love you."

"I'm sorry," Bradley says, "but you did this to yourself."

The sun melts into the jagged line of the mountains. I watch the men limp back to the ward. I try to crawl after them, but my body feels weighted by wet sand. My flesh pools into the earth. Air squeezes from my lungs. My bladder wrings out its contents. Above me the sky grows cluttered with stars. The ward's windows are stark squares of light in the deepening gloom. Sam will arrive soon and begin making his rounds, strapping the men into their pods. I dare to hope he will notice I'm missing. But the men have probably planned this part too. They will simply close my pod's lid and tell Sam they've already tucked me in for the night.

Coyotes wail in the distance. Soon they will find me and sink their teeth into my boneless body. I hope that my bones will reconstitute inside them at sunrise, piercing their organs, killing them. My eyes sparkle with their own starlight and I know I am about to pass out from the pressure on my brain. I comfort myself with unlikely scenarios. Maybe the coyotes will be repulsed by the smell of my excretions. Maybe my bones will form again in just the right way, skull not slicing through brain, ribs not lancing heart. I survived many nights, after all, before coming to the Bone Ward.

The coyotes howl closer now. The wind raises whorls of dirt, filling my open mouth with tiny stones. The walls of my lungs suck against each other. My heart struggles to fill its chambers. Darkness, silence, a pit without walls. Into the void of the boneless night, I let myself fall.

CORPSE FLOWER

BY LUCY TAN

DANA CALLED ME CORPSE Flower—*Titan Arum*, when she was being fancy about it. Her mother collected exotic flowers from around the world, and Dana named me after this one because it's a late bloomer. When it does bloom, it gives off a scent of rotting flesh and its spadix sticks out like a penis. She, Meg, Allie, and I stood around her family's greenhouse, daring one another to touch it.

"Go ahead, Corpse," she said to me. "Give it a hand job."

There were other late bloomers she could have named me after, but she chose this one because she said the flower and I have something creepy in common. There's nothing creepy about me. I'm sensitive—or imaginative—or something else Dana doesn't understand.

"Spunk Machine, you're up," she said to Allie, when I shook my head and stepped back. "Show her how it's done."

We have only ever seen the *titan arum* flower once, because it takes seven to ten years to bloom. The bloom lasts a couple days, and then it could be another seven to ten years before it happens again. In all that time, it just sits there sucking up the hothouse heat so that when it's ready the warmth will trick insects into thinking it's fresh meat. When I told the other girls this fact, they said it was disgusting. But I liked the idea of the corpse flower pretending to be another species, and I regretted not touching it when I had the chance. I think I could have felt something the other girls couldn't—a spark of understanding.

Dana gave each of us nicknames to prove that we were close to her. We were Beandip, Spunk Machine, Corpse Flower, and Spaztastic. We tried to call her something back, but nothing ever stuck. Dana was just Dana. Even the kids from East Orange High knew her as that, no last name necessary. When we walked into the Wendy's where they hung out after school, they were all, "Hey, look, it's Dana and the Rich Girls," like we were some '70s band.

We weren't from East Orange. We were from Short Hills, a few exits down, where kids spent their afternoons in test prep and all the teachers had Ivy League degrees. But my friends weren't like that—we'd rather leave town. One of the EO guys, DK, knew the manager at the Wendy's on the freeway and could get our Frosties spiked with rum. I wasn't straight but I didn't drink much, either, and when DK handed me mine it was like he knew. "Don't look so stressed," he'd say, winking. I hated being called out like that. The big worry was that nobody from our town had any edge anymore, and I didn't want to be grouped with the people we'd left behind.

DK was a couple years out of EO High but didn't look it—still wore his hat low, sneakers bright white and untied. I knew that when Dana talked about "edge" she was talking about him and his friends, because there was something about the way they spoke to us at the parties they threw—"You sure you're having fun?"—that made their words feel multidimensional. Like if you were to run your finger along the other side of their meaning, you wouldn't like what you found there.

At DK's, the adults were never home. They seemed to have been plucked from that house without notice, leaving a lot of unfinished business: an unopened package of XL boxer briefs sitting on top of a pile of mail, a kitchen window taped over with black plastic that huffed in and out with the wind. Once, in their bathroom, I found the top half of a pair of false teeth lying on the floor by the trash. It was furred with mold in the trench where the gums go. Our parents weren't home much either, but they were executives. Used to managing things from afar. Through the telephone, we could hear their rolling suitcases, the soft babble of hotel-room TVs. We believed in them like we believed in God. There was no proof they could protect us from anything, but it was nice to have someone to call on.

"I don't like it here," I said to Meg that night, coming out of DK's bathroom. "I feel like something bad's gonna happen."

She shushed me. "Don't say that so loud. They already think we're snobs."

A scream came from the living room. By the time we got out there, people were huddled around the couch, shaking a guy whose eyes had rolled into the back of his head. The shaking wasn't necessary, because when they let go, the guy was shaking all on his own. DK called an ambulance and kicked everyone out. "That was creepy," Meg said as we walked down the street, trying to decide what to do with ourselves. But she wasn't talking about what had happened—she was talking about the fact that I had known something would.

*   *   *

When summer came, Dana started dating DK, which pretty much meant the rest of us were dating him too. He drove us around in different cars, some that rode new and smooth, some with busted engines and bent tailpipes. He never had anywhere to be. When we asked him what he did for work, he said he was a bookie. When we asked what that meant, he said he was in the business of breaking bones.

"Like a hit man?"

"Well," he said, "not really."

DK was 5'8" and wiry. If he was in the Mafia, we figured him to be on the strategy end of things. But later that day he said he had something to show me.

"Stand like this."

He slid his hands down my calves and pulled my feet apart, thumbs hooked around my insteps. "Lean forward. Now put your weight on the balls of your feet."

Across the room, Dana watched us with unease. This was her first boyfriend. She couldn't be sure, but she sensed there were some lines being crossed.

I had a good view of DK's head; it was shaved, with little green dots where the hair used to be. "If you're small, you have to be fast. Gotta get the guy like *this*." He backed up and lunged at me from the side, throwing me over his shoulder. From where I hung upside down, I could see Dana frowning.

"Badass," she said. "Do you give piggyback rides too?"

Dana never used to be sarcastic, but her mind now bent this way. Small change, compared with her body's recent developments. There were now greater dimensions to Dana that DK was helping to explore. They explored in private and in our company: behind the school gym, in the woods, in the blocked-off wing of the library overlooking the bridge. Underneath the bridge, they giggled and lost their balance and tried not to trample the trash that filled the dried-up creek.

He had maybe been to jail—that's why the rest of us liked him. In Dana's words, he was "a Collector with a capital C." She said it with one eyebrow kinked, in a way that made her look vaguely famous.

"Yeah, right," I said, not because I didn't believe her but because her sarcasm was catching.

"You've seen his bruises. And last night some guy couldn't pay, so he had to shoot him in the knee."

Meg's jaw dropped at this; a bite of sandwich unstuck itself from the roof of her mouth. The rest of us flicked the tabs on our soda cans, did our best to ignore Dana's lunch-table celebrity.

"Do bookies even exist anymore?" Allie finally asked. "Don't people do that kind of thing online?"

"You can't punch someone through the internet, genius," Dana said.

None of us knew much else about DK, but my sister, Monica, had opinions. She was three years ahead of us, "away" at college but not far enough to stay there. Most weekends she was back home doing very Monica things like washing organic lettuce in the kitchen and drying it on paper towels. She had a condescending way of pulling a square off the roll.

"Oh, I know that guy," she said. "He was in my year, but at EO. Made friends at all the neighboring schools, and then dropped out halfway through. Goes around telling people he's spent time in China learning martial arts and stealing cars down in Key West. But if you want to know what *I* think"—lettuce bones crunched beneath her palms—"I think he never went anywhere at all. I think there's trouble at home."

Monica and I are completely different, but when she's around the house, the differences get blurred. It's hard to distinguish between her stuck-up-ness and my caution, her judgment and my intuition, her need for control and my need for control. I worry that my friends see too much of her in me.

"Stop thinking," Allie said later, when we were back in my room. "Close your eyes if you have to."

She rolled up my sleeve while Dana approached with the sewing needle, all sterilized and dipped in India ink. I closed my eyes and imagined being some other version of myself, one who is prepared for the things I want.

"*Ow*," I said, before the needle even got close. "Just hold on," I told them. "Just give me a minute."

It was fall again. Dana, Meg, Allie, and I stood outside my house shivering in our pajama pants, the tops rolled down into thick flannel lips. We squinted at the road, listening to the leaves shifting around on people's lawns and waiting for DK to pull up louder than he had to. It took a while for him to come, and in that time a presence gathered around us.

"Shh," I said. "Did you hear that?"

"Man, everything freaks you out, doesn't it?" said Dana, jealous that the dark talks only to me. I could see my friends exchanging looks, the darting whites of their eyes. They were starting to match, from the way they stood with their hips out to the homemade tattoos healing on their forearms. All I had was a smattering of birthmarks that I still sometimes connected into the shape of Ursa Minor with a ballpoint pen.

Dana's sleeve was pushed up so her tattoo shone in the moonlight. She'd chosen the infinity symbol—another way of saying she was limitless. But I'd seen her more scared than she could admit. I was the one she came to after getting the piercing that made her tongue swell up to the size of a baby bird. And then there was that time the two of us walked to CVS and back twice before she bought the Pill. She distracted us the whole while with the *other* thing she had done the night before. How she had nicked the keys to her dad's Camaro and let DK drift the two of them down Edgemere Avenue—clutch, brake, twist, twist, twist—like it was no big deal to let someone else have control of your life like that. It took me a while to figure out why I was the one she came to when she messed up. It wasn't because I was nice to her, and it wasn't because I was the best person to help. It was because she looked at me and thought, At least I'm really living.

There were a lot of people in DK's basement that night. We didn't all fit on the couches, so Meg, Allie, and I were sitting on the floor while Dana was sitting in DK's lap. Someone had switched the TV to a porn station that DK's dad got for free after paying the cable guy a little something on the side.

"That girl's a C," DK said idly, gesturing toward the TV.

"I don't know," Dana said, looking down at her own chest.

"No question. Thirty-four C." To the rest of us he added, "I used to work at Victoria's Secret."

Onscreen, the woman's breasts jumped up and down like puppies trying to lick her chin. I watched the boys' faces, their range of expressions. "Pick one, any one," Dana had once said to me. What she really meant was: *Don't you know how powerful it is to be a girl?* I looked over at DK, and when I caught his eye I did a thing I'd never done before: I didn't let go.

An hour later I was on the front steps waiting, thinking about women in their bodies, when DK finally came outside to stand next to me. He was holding two jackets: one pink, the other green. He dropped the pink one on my head and I said, "That's not my coat." He put the other one on and said, "Ain't mine either." We walked out to his car, but before we got in he put his hand on my shoulder. "I want you to know something. I didn't steal this. The car, I mean. This one's mine."

"Okay," I said, but when I got inside, the seats did feel a little expensive. And I thought, Maybe I do want to do something dangerous. I wondered if DK was grading me underneath the jacket and if he cared that I had straight As.

"So you wanna?" he asked.

"Wanna what?" I asked back, even though I had a pretty good idea.

He nodded toward the house, where Dana might be watching.

"You wanna learn how to steal?"

His mouth parted cold and tasted the way plants smell. It was the first time I'd taken something that wasn't mine, and I didn't know what to do with it. But there are nights when your future seems to be daring you to change course. So you do or say something you don't mean, strain to listen for an echo of the person you might be.

I pressed harder into DK's mouth. He jerked back, put a hand to his face. The garage light sensed motion and came on, showing a pale green bruise on his jaw that matched the color of his hairless head.

"How'd you get that?" I asked.

"Some guy from a biker gang punched me while I wasn't looking."

The gray squiggles in his irises looked coiled and ready to spring. At the end of his right eyebrow were two pink bumps—the scars of an old piercing. He was staring not at me but past me, and when I turned I saw nothing except our two faces reflected in the car window. He held his face all tough, his chin tucked. Talking not to me but to the image of himself.

"My sister says she knows you," I told him.

"What's her name?"

"Monica," I said.

"Monica. I don't know any Monicas."

Of course he didn't. Know-it-alls are never the ones other people consider worth knowing. He started kissing me again, and there beyond the glass, the different versions of him closed in on us—the Victoria's Secret clerk, the car thief, the martial artist, the bookie. The garage light went off, taking our reflections with it.

"How does that feel?" DK asked me, his hand hot on my thigh. "Do you like it like this?"

We were going so fast that I definitely did not. But I imagined a corpse flower big enough to swallow that car—its petals rising up, trapping us inside. There was something dark and ripe that made me drop my seat back and let DK climb over the console. I felt the roughness at the nape of his neck and his breath on mine. The problem with taking things slow, with taking them right, is the fear that you'll miss them altogether. I'd spent my life waiting for these exact conditions to align. For moving forward to be less terrifying than being left behind.

HOYT AXTON IS FROM OKLAHOMA, AND SO IS ROGER MILLER

BY JOANNA HOWARD

an excerpt from Rerun Era

NO ONE IT SEEMS is from Oklahoma except for us and then I grow up and realize everyone is from Oklahoma they just don't talk about it after a certain point or no one talks about them? Cartoons are not encouraged in my home. They are silly and inane. But then there is the VHS, and that is something on my own time, so cartoons are permitted. Everyone can do what they want, I have the VHS! I am at one with the VHS! I watch Robin Hood the cartoon, and it is totally okay! All the characters are animals, and there are even mice in tea dresses, and there is the rooster who strolls and sings about Nottingham even though he has a drawl. What is this drawling rooster doing in Nottingham, I wonder?

And my mom even sits in the room with me for part of it because the strolling rooster is Roger Miller, and she loves Roger Miller despite all his songs being inane, and even while the rooster is strolling and whistling she starts in on 'trailers for sale or rent…' and goes on singing for a while, but does anyone say he is from Oklahoma? They do not. Who is from Oklahoma? I wonder. Is anyone? Is anyone famous from Oklahoma?

We sit there and we watch The Rockford Files! We watch it religiously, but does anyone tell me James Garner is from Oklahoma? They do not!

Who is from Oklahoma? Maybe murderers? Possibly thieves? Dipshit conservatives? Racists?

I don't find out about Woody Guthrie till I go to college! Till college! And even though we watch all the western movies at home, and I know Ben Johnson is a famous trick rider, I don't know he's from Oklahoma until college! And then in college I drive every weekend back and forth through Yale, Oklahoma because it's on my route, and I am hyperaware of Yale because it is a notorious speed trap, and I even get pulled over in Yale but do not get a ticket, because in those days (and still sometimes) I can bat eyes and act dumb and get out of a speeding ticket if the cop is a guy, and through all those travails with Yale, Oklahoma I never know that Chet Baker is from Yale, Oklahoma. Not for years. But where were all those people when I was growing up? I am a grown-up already when one of my friends tells another of my friends, within earshot, 'You have to meet her dad. He is like all the best things about Oklahoma.' She is talking about my dad. It is the first time I have thought good things about Oklahoma and about my dad at the same time, and I am grown already.

But I remember Della and the Dealer when Hoyt Axton plays it on an episode of WKRP in Cincinnati wearing a polyester western suit that is too small for him.

My dad loves Hoyt Axton. I do not. I think he is not so attractive. He's fat and he wears too-small western clothes and his hair is gray. I love Dr. Johnny Fever because I love rock and roll, and because I love Jim on Taxi best, because I already love people who seem fried, and have wild hair, and a hippie-type look, and who are wearing jean jackets and dark glasses. At five I love someone fried? They seem more real to me. Johnny Fever wears sunglasses indoors. He always seems hung-over. I love Venus Flytrap, too, even though I have never seen a black person except on TV. Venus wears the Porter Wagoner suits but with more style, I think, as if there were only one step between the Porter Wagoner suits and Venus Flytrap suits. There are so many steps! But how would I know, because in Oklahoma we don't totally get it about Super Fly suits, even though my dad is liberal because of being a teamster, and he votes for Jesse Jackson when he runs for candidate, and he enjoys Redd Foxx very much, and we watch Sanford and Son in reruns every day, and sometimes dad listens to the albums by Redd Foxx, and also listens to the Richard Pryor albums, in the same way my brother listens to the George Carlin albums, and I get the impression that things coming out of the record player that are not music but are talking are just way raunchy, because I am often repeating these things with enthusiasm and having my mother say, 'Don't talk raunchy.' I also get the impression that elsewhere in the world there are black people making words and records and movies and TV, they just aren't from Oklahoma, or anywhere around close (and it is not till college that I find out that Ralph Ellison is from Oklahoma City and Langston Hughes is from Joplin, and although, yes, Joplin's in another state, still, we go there for everything, and I have never seen a black person there, and definitely not a famous black poet. What is going on?).

Both my dad and I love WKRP. Is it nice when my dad and I like the same things? I don't know. I don't know about that. I don't love Hoyt Axton, I know that. He is looking fat in that western suit. I also don't love sports, which my dad watches a lot of the time. Sports are the most boring and most cacophonous of all things. Our half house is not big enough for all that sound all the time.

I know that when I am in high school, and my friend who is older is over and is playing Steppenwolf and The Pusher comes on and he cranks it up so that you can hear the stereo all the way to the street, my mom and my dad come in from watering the lawn and throw a fit and fall in it because the neighbors are hearing the word 'goddamn' coming from the house at about 11. It just sounds better that loud. I don't think we any of us know it is a Hoyt Axton song. Because we none of us knew he was from Oklahoma, or talked about it.

My brother knew, I think, because he says, later, in a dead pan way: 'That's a Hoyt Axton song.'

Did he say that? I don't remember. It is much later, in that time when I am looking everything up, like crazy, because I'm scared I'm losing my memory of this place. I want to look it all up and have it confirmed in my mind. Otherwise, you forget.

Then I realize looking it up is what makes you forget. It just erases the memory.

Rerun Era *will be available October 2019 from McSweeney's Books.*

MARCUS BURKE graduated from the Iowa Writer's Workshop. Burke's debut novel, *Team Seven*, was published in 2014 by Doubleday. *Team Seven* received a starred review from *Kirkus Reviews*, was long-listed for the 2015 PEN Open Book Award, and was one of the "17 Books You Won't Be Able to Put Down This June" in *0, The Oprah Magazine*. Burke was the inaugural Creative Writing Fellow at Susquehanna University from 2016 to 2017, and is on the faculty at Southern New Hampshire University's Mountainview Low-Residency MFA program. He is currently at work on another novel.

PELLE CASS is a photographer from Brookline, Massachusetts. His work is in the collections of the Fogg Art Museum, the Addison Gallery of American Art, the Polaroid Collection, the DeCordova Museum, the Peabody Essex Museum, the MFA, Houston, and others. He has shown at the George Eastman House, the Albright Knox Gallery, the New Mexico Museum of Art, and the Metamorf Biennial for Art and Technology in Norway. Cass's work has been published widely online, in magazines, and in books, and he's received fellowships from Yaddo, the Polaroid Collection, and the Artist's Resource Trust.

ALEXANDER CHEE is the author of *How to Write an Autobiographical Novel*.

STEPHEN DIXON is the author of the story collections *Dear Abigail and Other Stories* (Trnsfr, 2018) and *Writing, Written* (Fantagraphics Books, 2019).

EMMA COPLEY EISENBERG's fiction and nonfiction have appeared in *Granta*, *Tin House*, *VQR*, *American Short Fiction*, the *Los Angeles Review of Books*, *AGNI*, and other publications. She lives in Philadelphia, where she co-directs the community literary hub Blue Stoop. Her first book, *The Third Rainbow Girl*, will be published by Hachette Book Group in 2020.

KATE FOLK's fiction and essays have appeared most recently in *Zyzzyva*, the *New York Times Magazine, Prairie Schooner*, and *One Story*. She lives in San Francisco and is working on a novel about AI limbs and emotional unavailability.

JOANNA HOWARD is a writer and translator from Miami, Oklahoma. Her memoir, *Rerun Era*, is forthcoming from McSweeney's in October of 2019. She is the author of the novel *Foreign Correspondent*, the story collections *On the Winding Stair* and *In the Colorless Round*, and *Field Glass*, a collaborative novel written with Joanna Ruocco. She also co-translated *Walls* by Marcel Cohen and *Cows* by Frédéric Boyer. She teaches in the literature PhD program at Denver University.

R.O. KWON's first novel, *The Incendiaries*, was published by Riverhead Books. She is a National Endowment for the Arts Literature Fellow. Her writing has appeared in the *Guardian*, *Vice*, *BuzzFeed*, *Noon*, *Time*, *Playboy*, and elsewhere.

RAVEN LEILANI has been published in *Narrative*, *Granta*, *New England Review*, and the *Florida Review*. She is the fiction editor of *Ruminate* magazine and an MFA candidate at NYU.

GORDON LISH is best known for his long labor as a strict destructionist, the latest book-length evidence of which posture is on exhibit in White Plains, New York. He is also a sucker for certain styles of liquid alliteration.

T KIRA MADDEN is an APIA writer, photographer, and amateur magician. She is the founding editor in chief of *No Tokens* and the author of *Long Live the Tribe of Fatherless Girls* (Bloomsbury, 2019). She lives in New York City and teaches at Sarah Lawrence College.

PETER McGRATH lives in a small, old house outside of Washington, DC, with a large, young cat.

JOSÉ ORDUÑA's work explores living as a racialized subject of the United States. His first book, *The Weight of Shadows: A Memoir of Immigration and Displacement*, was published in 2016 by Beacon Press. He is an assistant professor of English at the University of Nevada, Las Vegas.

JOSEPH OSMUNDSON is a scientist, teacher, and writer from a small town in Washington State. He has a PhD in molecular biophysics from the Rockefeller University, and his work has been published in places like *Guernica*, *BuzzFeed*, *Gawker* (RIP), the *Village Voice* (OMG RIP), and the *Feminist Wire*, where he works on the editorial staff. He's published two (award-losing) books and, with three other queer writers, co-hosts the "popular" podcast Food 4 Thot, a round-table discussion of books, boys, butts, and Beyoncé.

JACK PENDARVIS won two Emmys for his work on the television show *Adventure Time*.

ASALI SOLOMON is the author of *Disgruntled* and the story collection *Get*

Down. She lives in the city of Philadelphia, where she is currently working on another novel about Philadelphia.

SHRUTI SWAMY's fiction has been included in the 2016 and 2017 editions of *The O. Henry Prize Stories*, and has appeared in the *Paris Review*. She lives in San Francisco.

LISA TADDEO is a two-time recipient of the Pushcart Prize. Her debut book of nonfiction, *Three Women*, is out this summer from Simon & Schuster, to be followed by her first novel and story collection.

LUCY TAN is author of the novel *What We Were Promised*, available now from Little, Brown and Company. Originally from New Jersey, she currently lives in Wisconsin, where she is the 2018–19 James C. McCreight Fiction Fellow at the University of Wisconsin, Madison. She can be found at www.lucyrtan.com.

JENNY TRAIG spends most of her time at home with her family and her yarn stash. Her latest book is *Act Natural: A Cultural History of Misadventures in Parenting*.

LAURA VAN DEN BERG's most recent book is *The Third Hotel*. She is also the author of the novel *Find Me* and two story collections, including *The Isle of Youth*. Laura lives in Cambridge, Massachusetts, where she is a Briggs-Copeland Lecturer in Fiction at Harvard.

COLIN WINNETTE is the author of several books, including *The Job of the Wasp* (Soft Skull Press) and *Haints Stay* (Two Dollar Radio). He lives in San Francisco.

AVAILABLE FROM McSWEENEY'S

store.mcsweeneys.net

NONFICTION

VOICE OF WITNESS

ALL THIS AND MORE AT

store.mcsweeneys.net

HANNAH VERSUS THE TREE
by Leland de la Durantaye

"Hannah Versus the Tree *is unlike anything I have ever read—*
thriller, myth, dream, and poem combined." —James Wood

ALL THAT IS EVIDENT IS SUSPECT
Readings from the Oulipo 1963-2018

Edited by Ian Monk & Daniel Levin Becker

ALL THAT IS EVIDENT IS SUSPECT:
READINGS FROM THE OULIPO, 1963–2018
edited by Ian Monk & Daniel Levin Becker

The first collection in English to offer a life-size picture of the group in its historical and contemporary incarnations, and the first in any language to represent all of its members

Small Blows Against
Encroaching Totalitarianism

Volume Two   The Manifesto Series
McSweeney's Books

SMALL BLOWS AGAINST ENCROACHING TOTALITARIANISM, VOLUME TWO
edited by McSweeney's

*Gathered here are twenty-two pieces in which powerful voices, from poets
and novelists to actors and activists, speak to our predicament, to their state
of mind, and to the crucial importance of committing to take action.*

THE BOATBUILDER
by Daniel Gumbiner

Long-listed for the 2018 National Book Award

"Told with wit and heart, The Boatbuilder *is a meditation on love,
loyalty, and the shared experiences that turn strangers into family."*
—Tayari Jones

Founded in 1998, McSweeney's is an independent publisher based in San Francisco. McSweeney's exists to champion ambitious and inspired new writing, and to challenge conventional expectations about where it's found, how it looks, and who participates. We're here to discover things we love, help them find their most resplendent form, and place them into the hands of curious, engaged readers.

THERE ARE SEVERAL WAYS TO SUPPORT MCSWEENEY'S:

Support Us on Patreon
visit *www.patreon.com/ mcsweeneysinternettendency*

Volunteer & Intern
email *eric@mcsweeneys.net*

Subscribe & Shop
visit *store.mcsweeneys.net*

Sponsor Books & *Quarterlies*
email *amanda@mcsweeneys.net*

To learn more, please visit *www.mcsweeneys.net/donate* or contact Director Amanda Uhle at *amanda@mcsweeneys.net* or 415.642.5609.

All donations are tax-deductible through our fiscal sponsorship with SOMArts, a nonprofit organization that collaborates with diverse artists and organizations to engage the power of the arts to provoke just and fair inclusion, cultural respect, and civic participation.

NEW WORK BY

ALEXANDER CHEE
LAURA VAN DEN BERG
R.O. KWON
T KIRA MADDEN
GORDON LISH
EMMA COPLEY EISENBERG
JOSÈ ORDUÑA

PHOTOGRAPHY BY
PELLE CASS

AND MUCH
MORE

ISBN 978-1-944211-66-0

$24.00